Praise for The Memoirs of a Beautiful Boy

"*The Memoirs of a Beautiful Boy* is a wonderful book—tender, funny, and intelligent. . . . Leleux is possessed of remarkable wit and timing."　　　—*Houston Press*

"[A] funny-faced, sad-eyed beauty of a book—this generation's *Breakfast at Tiffany's*."　　—*Washington Blade*

"Leleux's story is a joyful read. Like David Sedaris, he . . . cheekily dispenses bons mots about everyday life."
　　　　　　　　　　　　—*Rocky Mountain News*

"Leleux proves he's already a master of the snappy one-liner and the improbably hilarious in this rollicking, bittersweet (emphasis on the bitter) coming of age memoir. . . . Not for the timid, this laugh-out-loud tale of dysfunction and discovery is a compulsively readable treat; any fan of Augusten Burroughs or David Sedaris owes it to themselves to pick it up."
　　　　　　　　　—*Publishers Weekly* (starred review)

"[Leleux] displays a nice self-effacing wit, a talent for constructing scenes, and a genuinely sweet spirit that engages the reader's sympathy."　　　　—*Booklist*

"An outrageous, raunchy ride, filled with pages of bend-over funny writing."　　　—*In Los Angeles* magazine

The
Memoirs
of a
Beautiful Boy

The Memoirs of a Beautiful Boy

~ ★ ~

ROBERT LELEUX

St. Martin's Griffin ✻ New York

www.stmartins.com

The Library of Congress has catalogued the hardcover edition as follows:

Leleux, Robert.
    The memoirs of a beautiful boy / Robert Leleux.—1st ed.
        p. cm.
    ISBN-13: 978-0-312-36168-6
    ISBN-10: 0-312-36168-8
    1. Mothers and sons—Anecdotes. 2. Authors, American—21st century—Family relationships. 3. Young gay man—United States. 4. Texas—Humor.
I. Title.
    PS3612.E44 Z46 2008
    813'.6—dc22
    [B]

                                                    2007039257

ISBN-13: 978-0-312-36169-3
ISBN-10: 0-312-36169-6

First St. Martin's Griffin Edition: January 2009

10 9 8 7 6 5 4 3 2 1

For Mother and Michael

A NOTE TO THE GENTLE READER;
OR ALWAYS TRUE TO YOU, DARLING,
IN MY FASHION . . .

This is the story of my Texas life. And while (essentially) true to my experience, I must warn that it often reads better (as in funnier, or happier) than it was lived. This service I've performed not merely for the sake of your sensibilities, but also for my art. After all, how does the old song go? *A hat's not a hat till it's tilted.* Well, mea culpa, I have tilted hats throughout, and certain names, places, details, and dates have been changed or condensed to avoid identification with real persons or events. I have also, naturally, corrected unbecoming camera angles, softened direct, overhead lighting, altered outmoded skirt lengths, reduced unflattering early-morning, under-eye puffiness, bloating, and splotchiness, as well as reversing the accelerated aging effects of excessive exposure to ultraviolet rays. For this & all, *mes petites*, forgive me.

CONTENTS

One must suffer in order to be beautiful.
—French proverb

To say that every Texan is a millionaire is just a tiny
little bit of an exaggeration. For instance, they have
"only" 125,000 millionaires in Houston. And nearly two
million non-millionaires.
—Miroslav Sasek, *This Is Texas*

The
Memoirs
of a
Beautiful Boy

Something New

*I*n the Dear John letter Daddy left for Mother and me, on a Saturday afternoon in early June 1996, on the inlaid Florentine table in the front entry of our house, which we found that night upon returning from a day spent in the crème-colored light of Neiman's, Daddy wrote that he was leaving us because Mother was crazy, and because she'd driven me crazy in a way that perfectly suited her own insanity.

We'd just been to the Dairy Queen. My mouth was full of hamburger when I found the letter. Mother still had on the Jackie O sunglasses I'd given her earlier that week for her forty-fifth birthday, and was fumbling on the wall for the light switch. I read through the letter once, fast, and then called to Mother, who read it over slowly, sitting down in one of the low white chairs that lined the hall. Mother didn't sit as she typically sat, with her calves fixed before her like they were the pillars of her lap. The way Mother sat on the low white chair against the wall of the entry, willowy leaves of yellow legal paper drifting from her thin fingers, her calves looked as though they'd collapsed. She signaled with the letter to the shopping bags beside the front door, their tissue paper poking up like dorsal fins: "All that goes back tomorrow."

My first reaction to Daddy's leaving was relief. I was sixteen, and what I wanted most for my mother was a divorce. For years, I'd kept a stack of Mother's old magazines under my bed, copies of *Vanity Fair* and *Hello!*, with dog-eared articles about Pamela Harriman, and ladies for whom the end of marriage was only the beginning of plastic surgery and happy new lives.

One afternoon, while watching *Of Human Bondage* on the Channel 13 *Three O'Clock Million Dollar Movie*, when Bette Davis told Leslie Howard, "It made me sick when I let you kiss me. . . . I used to wipe my mouth!" Mother said to me, "Hmm. That's pretty much the way I feel about your father."

So my dream was for Mother to leave Daddy. Then we could escape Nana and Papa's horse ranch outside Petunia, a small town the settlers managed to chop out of The Great Piney Woods of East Texas a hundred miles north of Houston. Between the freeway being rerouted and the recent construction of a Super Wal-Mart outside town, Petunia wasn't much more than a Dairy Queen, some gas stations, and a funeral home. White-columned and stately, Kahn's Funeral Home on Main Street was, in fact, the prettiest thing about Petunia, which, in itself, was pretty depressing. "It figures you'd have to die in this town to experience beauty," Mother said.

Mother spoke in quotable phrases, as though she intended her words to be embroidered. One of her great pleasures was thinking up new ways to describe just how ugly our town was, and the way she'd settled on in the summer of 1996 was to say that Petunia was Where God Stuck The Enema. We lived in what Mother called our South Will Rise Again house, a Greek Revival creation that stank of new money and was practically lacy with pillars and columns and porticos and little moldings of cherubim flying all over the place. It sat in the middle of a flat, empty pasture on my grandparents' ranch, and in the summer our white house shone like a heat spot from the road.

With her divorce settlement, I dreamt that Mother would move us into a real neighborhood in the city of Houston, shady with fat, mossy live oaks; and I'd wear a blue-blazered uniform to St. John's or Kincaid, the city's swank prep schools, instead of attending the fundamentalist Lutheran school that was the best education Petunia had to offer. Once we'd moved, every day could be like our Saturdays at Neiman's, where Mother and I went to get our hair and nails done at the salon and then go shopping.

But in all the time I'd spent daydreaming about my parents' divorce, the idea had never occurred to me that Daddy, who looked like an Oscar in a baseball cap—six feet four, bald, and muscle-y, with skin permanently tanned golden brown from long days in the Texas sun—might leave my glamorous, blond Mother.

People thought she was a TV star. Shopgirls would say, "Aren't you that lady on TV?" By which they meant no one in particular. Sometimes somebody would say Barbara Eden. Sometimes Suzanne Somers. Occasionally Connie Stevens. It's not that Mother looked like these people—she just looked like someone special. Waiters at posh restaurants like Brennan's and Tony's often gave us free food, afraid Mother was a famous person they didn't recognize who might have them fired for offering less than VIP service. And though by forty-five, Mother's makeup had grown heavier to shade the tiny wrinkles around her eyes that looked like fractures in a windshield, men in pickup trucks still hung out of their windows to whistle at her on the freeway. "What makes me irresistible," Mother once asked me, wearing an expression like she'd swallowed sour milk, "to a man in a pickup truck and a baseball cap?"

Despite his Houston Astros cap and his old Dodge pickup, Mother would never have left my father. The reason she'd stayed with him, and the reason his leaving us meant bad trouble, was because Daddy, by himself, had no money. Which was something I always forgot while reading *Vanity Fair*. Daddy didn't have any money, because Papa, Daddy's rich father, had a *Bonanza* fantasy, to keep his son on his horse ranch at all costs. Nana and Papa paid Daddy a crazy-huge allowance throughout my parents' marriage, so he would stay on their ranch and use his vet degree to breed and doctor Papa's champion racehorses. They footed my parents' bills, bought Mother and Daddy's cars, and paid off their charge accounts. So, on paper, Daddy was a poor man. And our tacky white house was the only thing in the world my parents really owned, which meant that any divorce settlement would be pitifully small.

Some twenty years earlier, Daddy had fallen in love with Mother at a Steve McQueen movie at the Texas A&M student union, and they'd married while he was still in veterinary school. Mother had been a campus celebrity. She'd earned extra money modeling clothes on local television for Lester's department store—where her job had been to stare into the camera and whisper "Lester's" in a way that sounded mysterious and sexy. As a young girl at A&M, Mother had married Daddy, believing his rich parents would eventually make him rich, too, either by setting him up with a trust fund or a business to run. And when that hadn't happened, she'd stayed for Nana and Papa's money.

Mother let Daddy's letter fall to the floor, twisting her engagement ring around her finger. "Jesus God," she said. "This is a *pig fuck*."

"Pig Fuck" was Mother's phrase for the absolute nadir of something. Lycra was, for instance, the pig fuck of fabrics, with English toile, pimento loaf, Japanese cars, and Miracle Whip serving as further examples. And because Mother was an extreme person, whose circumstances tended to swerve from the best to the worst, our life involved lots of pig fucks. ("There is no such thing," she once told me, "as a *happy* medium.") As a small boy, I'd even seen Mother wrap her white mink around the rickety shoulders of a shivering girl waiting in a January slush outside the Petunia post office. And over the years, Mother had spent every dollar that passed through her checkbook on clothes, jewelry, and luxury vacations. So when Daddy left, taking Nana and Papa's money with him, Mother and I quickly realized we were nouveau poor. Which was the pig fuck of all time. "As of this minute, Robert," Mother said, "we have one hundred and twenty-seven dollars in the bank."

I started to feel queasy, as if the tomato aspic and tiny cucumber sandwiches Mother and I had eaten earlier that afternoon at Neiman's tearoom were reacting poorly with the Belt Buster I'd gotten at the Dairy Queen. "You're right," I told Mother. "This *is* a pig fuck."

Mother reread Daddy's letter a couple of times, then took off her heels, and shrank four inches in five seconds. "He just loves us *so* much he had to go right out and leave us. Well, I shouldn't be surprised. What can you expect when you cast pearls at swine?" Then Mother went to the kitchen, and filled an Evian bottle with vodka—something she often did when she was depressed but wanted to appear concerned with physical fitness. "I'm going to bed to watch my movie," she said.

I knew from long experience that *Breakfast at Tiffany's* was Mother's movie. The VCR was invented for my mother, because if something was good, then more of it was better. When Mother was fond of a movie, like *Breakfast at Tiffany's*, she couldn't watch it too many times. That VHS tape was among the great stabilizing influences of her life; she tended to fall back on it whenever her emotions swung too far in any direction, and particularly when she was depressed. That night, Mother looked like she needed *Breakfast at Tiffany's* badly.

I don't know what I'd expected in a letter from my father explaining the necessity of his leaving me, but Daddy's letter was, nevertheless, a disappointment. It filled four wandering, rumpled pages, in an ink too bright for its purpose, and was peppered with the same humdrum gripes that filled his regular fights with Mother. That Mother and I hated, and were abjectly humiliated by, his family. That she was never satisfied, and had taught me to be never satisfied, too, and that we both spent his money with disregard. "Nothing's ever good enough for you two," Daddy wrote, before starting a sputtering list of the various occasions he'd found our behavior odd, or, rather "unnormal." Daddy carped that Mother had become obsessed with preserving her youth and beauty. That she'd had her face lifted and hadn't told him; and that we'd spent his birthday in Rome, and their wedding anniversary in Paris, and hadn't even telephoned. But soon after Daddy began listing his grievances, the wattage of his fight fell low, and he shortly wound down to signing, "Your Loving Father and Husband, Bob O'Doole."

I was baffled. I couldn't imagine him writing such a letter. You could tell Daddy had taken his time in writing it, because sometimes the ink changed color, from blue to black, even in the middle of a sentence. Sometimes his handwriting was hard-pressed and jagged, sometimes faint, as though his words could hardly stand to touch the paper. I tried to imagine Daddy writing—angry, by the cab light of his old pickup that danced with diesel and George Jones songs, or sad, sitting in an empty bathtub in the middle of the night. But I couldn't, because in my whole life, I'd never seen him write anything longer than a check. And because, while Daddy had plenty of grounds for divorce, I found it deeply peculiar that he'd choose to leave us for a string of petty grievances, instead of one big, overarching outrage. Daddy had always seemed to have the lowest threshold for satisfaction of anybody I'd ever known. As long as he got to spend his days with Papa and the horses, I couldn't imagine him making big changes in his life, particularly something this drastic. He wasn't constantly distracted, like Mother and I, by desire. Daddy was living proof of the Buddha's claim that desire only makes you miserable, but he also proved *my* belief that desire is the only thing that makes you interesting. My father didn't want anything, and he was not interesting.

"Ahh," Daddy had sighed, when I told him, on the night Mother and I returned from our first trip to Manhattan, that when I grew up, I wanted to be a star of New York City; that I wanted to make best friends with Dina Merrill and Kitty Carlisle Hart (who were the two people I'd most often seen photographed in *Town & Country*, which was another magazine Mother subscribed to); and that I wanted us all to go tap dancing together under the Eloise portrait at the Plaza Hotel, singing "New York, New York" with Liza Minnelli while riding in a carriage through Central Park on our way to Bloomingdale's. "You'll grow out of all that," he said. And then he grinned. Daddy was a grinner. You could watch him idling across Papa's land, his Astros cap tipped back, and always that same dumb grin. "One day, you'll realize that everything good about life's right here. Just like George Bailey in *It's a Wonderful Life*." It drove me crazy whenever Daddy used *It's a Wonderful Life* as a parable. His whole life, he'd had one favorite color (blue, which is practically everybody's favorite color) and one favorite movie, *It's a Wonderful Life,* because it confirmed his perception of the world: that anything that really mattered could be found at your own front door, which in our case was in the middle of Papa's pasture.

So, as the next few days passed and we didn't hear from Daddy, I walked around in a state of furious disbelief, wondering how I could have gotten my father so wrong; how a man who seemed as satisfied as he did could suddenly pick up and leave his life. It was positively confounding. But then something happened that made me realize that in his letter Daddy hadn't expressed a forthright position. Something happened that made me understand that the reason he left Mother and me while we were gone to Neiman Marcus and the Dairy Queen had little to do with however *unnormal* we happened to be. Daddy decided to leave us because he'd found something new. And Something New was pregnant.

The following week, when Daddy brought Something New, brought Pam, to my mother's house to pick up his remaining things, a day Mother referred to as The Sacking of Troy, and Pam wore a draping man's flannel shirt that just revealed a bulging belly too firm for fat, it became quite clear that Daddy's departure wasn't nearly so sudden as it seemed, and that he'd considered it, at the very least, since February.

That afternoon Mother didn't go downstairs, insisting it was beneath her dignity to confront her husband's mistress in her own front hall. "If your father thinks he's going to humiliate me in front of That Woman, then he'd just better think again." I stayed upstairs with Mother, and we both peeked down, from a place on the landing where we knew we wouldn't be seen. "Let's see the merchandise they're peddling these days, Robert," Mother told me.

While my father rummaged, Pam waited in the front hall. Every part of her body was wiry and hungry looking, except for her huge stomach—which pooched out before her like a python that had swallowed a rabbit. "Look at her," Mother said, eyeing Pam's stomach. "Full as a money bag. Full as a deposit slip. . . .

"You know, you stay in a marriage," she said. "Even when you know it doesn't work, because . . . it works in the way it doesn't work. In a way that starting over . . . *from scratch* . . . does not work.

"Oh, Robert," said Mother, "it is time for me to start over *from scratch*."

CHAPTER TWO

Texas Blonde

Of course, there never would have been a convenient time for Daddy to leave us, broke, for his pregnant mistress. But even if we'd saved our money, or if we'd had some way of making some, June 1996 still would have been a pretty lousy time for Mother and me to start life over again from scratch. By then, Mother had resigned herself to the fact that the glamorous highlight of her life had been back at Texas A&M, modeling as The Lester's Girl on local television. And though it seemed like we were always zooming across Houston's freeways in Mother's white Jaguar, trying to think up excuses to spend as much time away from Nana and Papa's ranch as possible, there was an excitement in our attempts at escape.

On the morning of the Saturday Daddy would leave us, Mother and I woke up late and hadn't managed to miss the day's first wave of heat. The only time we felt generous toward the ranch was when we were leaving it, and on that morning, as the dew on Papa's Bermuda grass began to steam into the heavy, East Texas summer air, we'd almost been prepared to call it beautiful.

Mother's wig was crooked.

The bobby pins that held her real hair down had come loose because it was hot and her scalp was sweating. She'd been trying to mop up all the little sweat trickles by scratching at her wig, which made her whole fake head of blond hair slide forward, so her bangs were down in her eyes. Which made it difficult to drive.

Mother reached up, and opened the mirror on the sun visor, and puckered her lips and checked her lipstick, and then scraped her fingernail at a little stray dab of mascara that had been bothering her all morning long. She gave a good sweet look at herself and, managing to keep one hand on the steering wheel, yanked at the back of her head until her hairline receded a couple of inches. Then she jerked past the little red sports car that had been lagging along in the left-hand lane. Mother had been praying that the little red car's driver would drop dead of coronary arrest right there in the fast lane of the 610 loop: "Take him, Lord. Just take him." Because Mother believed that if you asked Jesus to kill somebody, fast, it wasn't a death curse. *Jesus* made it a prayer.

We were going to Neiman Marcus to get our hair and nails done. That's how we spent every Saturday morning. Mother had been born with completely decent hair—it was straight, honey brown, and plenty thick. But she'd been inspired in her teens by a thirties movie about some dull brunette who'd remade herself with a bottle of peroxide and a toothbrush in order to join the *Ziegfeld Follies*. So by the time I was born, when Mother was twenty-eight, her patchy scalp looked lethal, like a salt-sown garden or the coat of a mangy dog. And when she hadn't wound her hairs into tiny knots with bobby pins in order to have some foundation to keep her wigs secured to, weightless brown wisps of it floated off her head like wasps.

Going bald before thirty would probably cause the average woman to lose confidence. But, not Mother. Because she'd never really recovered from that moment, in the 1960s, when she was in high school and everybody wore hairpieces. When even if you had gushes of hair, you wore a hairpiece. Mother had never stopped filling out her hair with blond falls and switches and weaves, so when all her hair fell out, it just seemed like the next step. It just meant making the leap from partial to full-head wigs, and full-head wigs provided a more fantastic effect anyway. Which was perfect for Mother, because what she really wanted was fantasy hair. Maybe if Mother hadn't been such a beautiful woman, or if she hadn't preferred a simple style of dress, or hadn't possessed a basic cockiness and a sense of irony about her looks, then her wigs and pancake makeup would have made her look silly or sad. But this was Texas in the 1990s. Nobody had a sense of moderation. Mother looked fabulous.

Mother had a wall of cabinets built in her bathroom especially for her wigs. There were shelves of wigs on Styrofoam heads, sorted in rows by age, cut, and style. It looked like one of those cryogenic freezer vaults from the science-fiction movies where people have their heads preserved for posterity. "Morning, girls," Mother greeted her wigs, opening the cabinet doors to choose the day's hair.

Name a style, Mother had a wig for it. She had lots of winking Veronica Lakes and shoulder-length pageboys. Those were Mother's everyday wigs—good, versatile cuts, appropriate for various occasions, and capable of segueing, in a pinch, from day to evening. She had a few flips with heavy bangs, like Ann Marie on *That Girl*. This was Mother's Call In The Cavalry hair, and on mornings like this one, when Mother wore a flip, it meant she felt old and needed hair with some pep to it. Mother had several evening styles—high, towering folds of Gibson Girl hair that made her look like a sexy librarian. Eduardo, Mother's hairdresser at Neiman's, who had a hooked nose and smelled like canned peaches, dyed each of these wigs exactly the same color—a certain golden shade of blond that Mother loved, like an old, polished pocket watch. Gold, not yellow.

Since I had real hair and Mother didn't, she didn't even need to be in the room to have hers done—to get her wigs shampooed and set. So she always had time at the salon, while Raoul cut my hair and Eduardo finished with her wigs, which she usually used to get her brows shaped. Our hair appointment was for ten o'clock. It was always for ten o'clock, and it always took us an hour and a half to get from Petunia to Houston. But Mother always swore we could make it in less time, and so the last thirty minutes of our drive was enough to spook the horses. This was when Mother would start praying aloud for Jesus to just scoop away all the lazy, slow-moving cars to heaven, while flooring the accelerator so the wind from the freeway made her

Jaguar gasp and wobble like it was preparing to leave the ground. On that Saturday morning, we were, at 10:15, nowhere near Neiman Marcus.

And Mother and I were having the argument we usually had at 10:15 on Saturday morning. I was telling Mother that, of course, she didn't care if we were late, because she wasn't the one who had to deal with Harold, the receptionist at Neiman's salon—who was completely bald except for a little ponytail pulled together from the few remaining strands of hair that grew on the back of his head, which made him look like one of the little princes in *The King and I.* Harold complained we pushed his whole schedule back, and asked why we even bothered to make appointments if we intended to waltz in whenever we pleased? (But if it hadn't been that, it would have been something else, because Harold berated all of Neiman's customers, which Mother said was probably the reason he'd been hired in the first place—to convey to patrons their great good fortune in having been permitted to sidle through Neiman's sliding doors.)

"Not only do I have to deal with Harold," I continued, "but I'm the one who has to lug your wigs up three flights of escalators. I have to break my back carrying those heavy leather hatboxes, while you roam around the parking lot looking for a space, because even though you'll spend thirty-five dollars on a can of hair spray just because Eduardo recommends it, you won't spend five dollars to have your car parked."

Which was something that really drove me crazy about Mother—that her fondness for the lavish gesture tended to alternate, without warning, with an extreme chin-chiness when it came to little things like valet parking. Mother wouldn't valet-park. She'd only refill her gas tank at the spooky truck stop on the edge of town—with the attendant whose glass eye was a different color from his real eye, because gas there was a nickel cheaper a gallon than the Texaco station. And she'd only buy the off-brand toilet paper that felt like crushed glass it was so rough, and rather than buy dishrags, Mother made Juana, our housekeeper, cut her old lingerie into little towelettes, so that if you wanted to dry a fork or clean up a spilled puddle of Coca-Cola, you had to do it with a strip of chiffon that had a little frayed ribbon hanging off the end of it. "How about this," I offered Mother. "How about I, your sixteen-year-old son, pay to have your car parked, and you can tote your own Styrofoam heads upstairs."

Which led Mother to mention that I was usually a lot nicer by the time we'd gotten this close to a department store. "Try this, Robert," she suggested. "Why don't you try relating to me like I'm one of my credit cards?"

And the reason Mother and I could talk to each other this way, so that the meanest thing we could say was still funny and affectionate, was because we shared that special bond mothers share with their gay sons—even when they're only sixteen years old and don't know they're gay yet. Mother and I were best friends—a lucky thing, since besides each other, we were both utterly friendless. She had contempt for men, and didn't trust women, and I was a world-ranking sissy, and we were both isolated out on Nana and Papa's ranch. So among the only things I knew for sure, when I was sixteen years old, was that I adored my beautiful mother, and she understood me perfectly.

Mother thought her job as my parent was to make sure my life ended up as different from hers as possible—and she would have wanted me to get out of East Texas under any circumstances. But because I was gay, it seemed doubly important to take me to Neiman's, so I could learn to want more of everything. I think Mother considered homosexuality to be a form of aestheticism, and believed that by taking me shopping she was giving me a world where it would be easier to find my way than in the cowboy culture of Daddy's people. To Mother, Neiman Marcus was Gay School. Which was why she was willing to fight with Daddy every weekend when he wanted to take me with him to the Navasota Saturday Morning Live Cattle Auction.

Daddy's concern for me had developed early. By the time I could talk, he was correcting Mother when she brushed my hair and called me her beautiful little boy. "A boy isn't beautiful, Jessica," insisted my father. "He's handsome."

"*A boy* might be handsome," Mother answered. "But *my son* is gorgeous."

It was true that I was less handsome than beautiful, and true that I resembled the women in Mother's family more than any of the O'Dooles—a sore point with Daddy. I had the same blue eyes with gold flecks as Mother and my grandmother JoAnn—and their same high voice and heavy laughter. And I was so fair you could see veins running aquamarine beneath my skin, just like Mother and JoAnn. But these weren't the similarities that bothered Daddy most.

What really bothered Daddy were things like my learning lyrics off the rolls of JoAnn's player piano when I spent the night at her house in the Houston suburbs, and singing "Love for Sale" at her bridge parties—which JoAnn thought was adorable, because she'd read in a movie magazine that Vincente Minnelli taught Liza to sing "Love for Sale" at his parties, but which Daddy did not think was funny at all.

Counteracting all the Cole Porter I'd absorbed at my grandmother's was among Daddy's principal reasons for beginning my boxing training when I was six years old. He'd been a Golden Gloves champion—The Fighting Irish, they'd called him in the ring. His robe and trunks were made of green satin, with appliquéd shamrocks, and I don't believe that Papa—who carried spare boxing gloves behind the seat of his truck throughout my father's childhood so Daddy might wallop willing vagrants on the side of the road—ever forgave Mother for putting an end to my father's boxing when they'd first started dating in college. But on this issue, among many, Mother didn't care what Papa thought, since she believed boxing to be the first step down a short road toward becoming a white trash weirdo—a claim later substantiated by the fate of my cousin Willie, who was successfully trained by Papa, and who, by the time I was sixteen, lived in the woods and bred raccoons for a living: "I got a mama coon. I got a daddy coon. Pretty soon, they're gonna make me some baby coons."

So when Papa and Daddy put me in training they made me swear not to breathe a word of it to Mother. Which, despite my mortal terror, I agreed to, because Papa had found and met my price: I was a pony whore. Papa promised that if I fought Tito—the Mexican stable boy whose family lived in one of the service apartments behind the barns, and who often rode with me, wearing my castoff clothes, in our improvised merry-go-round (feed buckets hung from the electric horse-walker)—that a blond Shetland pony would be mine. So, in the early mornings while Mother was still sleeping, I trained with Papa, running laps in the copper red dirt of the horse barns. Tito, however, didn't require athletic training because his whole young life had been spent in violation of child-labor legislation, cleaning stalls and raking shavings. And no matter how thoroughly I absorbed the closest thing Papa had to a mantra, "Irishmen Don't Say Ouch," I knew that like most of The Poor, Tito could beat the bejesus out of me.

But even still, I kept my mouth shut, and my mind on the pony, because Papa guaranteed me that it didn't matter how pathetically I performed in the fight—as long as I stepped into the ring with Tito, and as long as I didn't cry or slap like a girl, he'd live up to our bargain. Which gave me an idea—resting largely on a skill I'd picked up with Mother while watching the Channel 13 *Million Dollar Movie.* So on the morning of our fight, when Papa and Daddy crowded the grooms and furrier around a blank patch of coppery dirt in a corner of the barn, and Tito charged forward to take his first swing at me, I swooned. I wafted, limp as a petal from the bloom, with a hand to my brow like I'd seen Bette Davis do.

It was my final moment of believing fainting to be one of those talents in the movies that people might be really impressed by, like singing operetta or tap dancing. An idea I was cruelly dissuaded from when, after a moment of dead quiet, Daddy began nudging my prone body with the toe of his boot, and Papa started slapping Daddy with his Stetson, and Tito looked genuinely perplexed, and I came to the sudden realization that nobody was buying me a pony. At which point, I revealed the whole foul scheme to Mother, who, taking my face in her hands, assured me Papa *would* buy me a pony.

For two glorious months after Prince was delivered to me dressed in a red ribbon halter, I rode him across Papa's pastures—until he was fried like rice under a pecan tree during a lightning storm. The next morning, as Mother and I watched one of Papa's grooms hitch Prince to the back of the tractor with a steel cable, and drag his stiff little corpse by his hind legs into the tall grass behind the racetrack, she asked me, "Do you want Papa to buy you another pony?" Mother crouched down to me, her high heels sinking into the dirt of the pasture.

"No," I said.

"Probably wise," Mother answered. "It's best to let the worst go."

Shortly thereafter, Daddy abandoned his dreams of my ever winning Golden Gloves. And the Cole Porter crisis ran its course when Mother cut off all communication with JoAnn after a big fight they had over, I believe, a surprise vacation my grandmother took to Acapulco. But it doesn't really matter what the fight was about since the root of their relationship was conflict. So by the time I was sixteen, I hadn't seen JoAnn in almost ten years, and my

cousin Willie's fate as a raccoon breeder had further convinced Mother of my need for male role models outside
my family—which led her to Neiman's. She thought it
was important for me to spend time around gay men like
Eduardo and Raoul, safely, while she was sitting next to
me getting her eyebrows waxed.

I loved our Saturdays at Neiman's for two reasons. The
first was that I had, without realizing it, developed a crush
on Raoul. He was the only longhaired man I'd ever known
who didn't look like Jesus or an antiwar protester, and
wore shirts so tight you could see his nipples. The way he
handled a blow-dryer made me tingle. And though I was
too naïve to understand this pleasure to be romantic, the
best five minutes of my week were when Raoul shampooed my hair.

The other reason I loved Neiman Marcus was because I
was pretty much convinced that I was Holly Golightly.
Since *Breakfast at Tiffany's* was Mother's favorite movie,
I'd watched it about a million times, and it seemed eerily
perfect that Holly was from Tulip, Texas, and I was from
Petunia. I wasn't fat, like Holly had been as a child, but I
did have a sense of myself as a hidden beauty. ("Doesn't
Robert have beautiful *features*," is what everyone besides
Mother tended to say about my looks, before remarking
upon my height, or high coloring, or the honey brown
hair and blooming lips I'd inherited from Mother and
JoAnn. Which led me to believe that my features might be
beautiful, but as a whole, the damn thing didn't quite
stick.) I was terrified that I might be a hayseed without
knowing it, and so I was constantly on the lookout for new

ways to transform myself. What Tiffany's was to Holly Golightly, Neiman Marcus was to me: the store that had everything you could ever want.

Neiman's was always a little dark, with uneven streaks of cream-colored light floating through the stained glass on the store's front wall, like milky ribbons in a cup of coffee before it's stirred. Neiman's salesgirls dressed in black. Silk scarves were folded behind polished sheets of glass. Perfumes, on gilt trays, smelled like spicy gardens. Linens were shiny white and lacy like a virgin's wedding dress. The sandwiches in the tearoom were cut in fragile wedges, and spread with French butter, and all the women's suits looked like smart, city women, who knew the Latin names for flowers, would wear them. I watched these women, to see which blouses they draped in front of themselves in the long mirrors hidden in the store's tall pillars, and which fragrances they allowed to be sprayed onto their wrists, or into the crooks of their arms after they'd pushed back their sleeves.

Mother had been absolutely determined that I'd grow up and become a star writer in New York City since I'd won first prize in the verse contest at Beckendorf Junior High School's arts competition, by composing a limerick inspired by an article I'd read in *Hello!*:

There once was a Princess named Di.
In her marriage she was living a lie.
She called her husband an armadilla,
And he ran off with Camilla.
And never a tear she did cry.

"Listen to that lyric," Mother had said at the time. "I suppose that's the reason to breed with shanty-Irish white trash. The poem. The muse. Someday you'll move to New York City, and you'll write all about me. You'll be my little Truman Capote."

Mother may have decreed that I would write when I was in junior high, but I decided to become a writer while listening in on ladies' conversations at the tearoom at Neiman Marcus. The English language never sounded smarter, more sparkling and lively, than when women gossiped and sparred while out to lunch with one another, and I wanted to grow up and write books that sounded just like them.

When I was sixteen years old, I was convinced that the hierarchy of angels had been glimpsed and copied at Neiman Marcus. *Maybe this is the universe's big bargain,* I remember thinking, noticing that people on Neiman's escalators seemed to float between floors. *Maybe the deal is that little African children have to starve and die, and others have to go blind making toys in China. Maybe I'll even get stuck in Petunia forever, living with my father's vulgar family, just so Neiman Marcus can look so beautiful. If that's how the world works, then it's almost worth it.*

The Blondie tape Mother had been listening to on the Jaguar's tape deck reached the end of side A, so she flipped it and turned up the volume to signal that it was time for me to stop complaining about how late she always made us, and to drown out the jet-plane sound of air coming through the windows. I put my bare feet up on the dashboard, and tried to read an article about Princess Caroline in the *Paris Match*, which I couldn't do because I couldn't read French. Mother couldn't read French either, but subscribed to the *Match* anyway because she liked the pictures of French dresses.

It was about ninety degrees outside. I was sweating, even though damp, mildew-y air was blowing strong out of the air conditioner. Staring into the blue summer sky outside the window, which was the thick crayon color of a Smurf, I tried to imagine that when I turned my eyes back to the ground it would vaguely resemble the French Riviera, where Princess Caroline seemed to be having a sordid affair, which was something I could guess without reading a word of French.

My stomach dropped and I felt queasy as Mother's car came bouncing over a dip in the freeway, and the tip of Neiman's rooftop became visible in the distance. I reached into Mother's huge calfskin purse and popped the lid off one of the Coca-Colas she always carried for me, taking a swig to settle my stomach. I loved that first moment when I could see Neiman's lazing among Saks and Hermès, like a lion patting back a yawn, and savored that part of our drive when downtown Houston's tall oil buildings stood as the backdrop to the swank, tailored stores of Post Oak, the city's shopping district. As Mother reached out for the Coke can, her charm bracelets jangled. She exited the freeway at San Felipe, and we began to descend to ground level.

"My wig straight?" Mother asked.

"Yeah," I said.

"How do I look?" she asked.

"You look beautiful." Mother did look beautiful in a tight silk dress. "And young," I said, successfully visualizing Mother as an American Express card in pantyhose. "You look very young today."

"Mm-hmm," Mother said, arching an eyebrow. She swerved into Neiman's parking lot, and then under the carport, so that the valet could park her car. Through the speakers, Blondie sang, sort of foggy because of the volume being turned up so high: *I'm not the kind of girl who gives up just like that . . .* Mother looked at me, and winked. "Happy?" she asked.

"Happy," I said.

CHAPTER THREE

All or Nothing

By the summer of 1996, Mother had pretty much given up on her dreams of leaving the ranch for a life of wealth and glamour. There had been a time, early in her marriage, when Mother—a woman born with tremendous style, but not one nickel—had quietly hated Daddy's parents for having failed to allow their new money to transform their material tastes and desires. But as Mother grew resigned to her life, she'd begun to hate my grandparents very loudly: "The only thing your grandparents' money has done for them is allow them to purchase white bread and Dr. Pepper in much larger quantities."

In fact, since an evening the previous April, when Mother had hated Nana particularly loudly, she hadn't even been on speaking terms with my grandparents. That spring evening, when Nana and Linda, Nana's Jehovah's Witness housekeeper, were celebrating a new way to bake biscuits, proved to be the last time Mother and I were to be invited over to my grandparents' house.

Going to Nana and Papa's redbrick house had always been a torture for Mother. Everything about the house, she claimed, was done in the worst possible taste. "As soon as white trash gets a little bit of money," Mother said, "they do one of two things. They either register in the Republican Party, or they buy a redbrick house. Your Nana and Papa, they did both."

In 1964, Nana and Papa owned a miserable little dairy on a couple of hundred acres just north of Houston, which they'd been lucky enough to buy with a huge mortgage thanks to the GI Bill. On the dairy, Nana and Papa's life had been one of hardscrabble poverty. Since they were too poor to hire help, my grandparents could seldom leave the dairy; their one hundred and fifty cows needed to be milked every twelve hours—so if they weren't milking cows, they were feeding cows, or herding cows, or slaughtering cows, or churning milk into butter.

At that time, Nana, Papa, Daddy, and my aunts Edie and Ida, lived in a two-room shotgun shack with a river of cow shit running through the front yard. Their house had been built on lower ground than the dairy barns, and Papa had jerry-rigged a sewage system so that every time a cow relieved itself the result was swept into a little canal that ran right out of the barns, through the front yard, and past the front door of their house. Daddy, Edie, and Ida were forever pushing or tripping one another into the river of cow shit, so that all three of them walked around the dairy oozing third-world infections that Nana "cured" with a black salve she mixed up with a wooden spoon in a galvanized tub in the backyard.

Then, one day, in the sort of stroke of luck usually reserved for characters in situation comedies, a man from Shell Oil Company drove up the road and asked to check the soil of my grandparents' dairy for natural gas deposits. Nana and Papa's dairy was, in fact, chock-full of natural gas deposits, and Shell Oil bought the dairy for millions of dollars. With his new money, Papa loaded up the truck and moved to Petunia. To Papa, the desolation of Petunia seemed like an opportunity. It was his chance to buy a big ranch in the middle of the country and live like the Cartwrights on *Bonanza*. But even in the days before the Super Wal-Mart bankrupted its small-business owners, Petunia was the sort of abandoned-looking place that strangers might drive straight through on their way to Dallas without ever realizing they'd passed a town at all.

So Papa bought a glamorous horse ranch with a covered swimming pool, a horse racetrack, ponds, and the big, red-brick house. Since everything Nana and Papa owned smelled like cow shit, Papa convinced the ranch's previous owners, the Florenzos, to sell him every stick of furniture, every piece of bric-a-brac, every sheet and towel in the place. When I was a child, it seemed strange to me that the Irish linen tablecloth, embroidered with little winged angels, that covered Nana's dining-room table was crowned with the Florenzos' monogram, but it pleased Papa to buy a rich man's stuff. Even at the time, it was obvious he was as proud that the Florenzos had *once* owned the ranch as he was of owning it himself.

In wealth, the O'Dooles followed their pleasure. Nana got fat off food that filled three refrigerators, and over the next twenty-five years Papa made himself famous throughout the state for breeding champion racehorses that ran the All-American Futurity. My aunts Edie and Ida married businessmen who owned other redbrick houses, and devoted their lives to making foods from recipes found in *McCall's* and *Family Circle*, like gelatin molds and casseroles, which tended to require ingredients like Coca-Cola and corn flakes. Papa dreamed his son would be the first O'Doole to go to college, so Daddy went to Texas A&M, where he met and married my beautiful mother, The Lester's Girl. "Why is it," she'd ask me, "that the works of culture our life most resembles are *Bonanza* and *The Beverly Hillbillies*?"

People called my grandfather "Preacher." Though he wasn't a minister, he'd earned the nickname while working as a roughneck in the Louisiana oilfields during the Great Depression. Papa said that while all the other roughnecks spent their paychecks on whores and liquor, he'd saved his money by marrying Nana. Mother always referred to this decision as a false economy. But it was enough to earn Papa his nickname—the standards for qualifying as a member of the clergy in the Louisiana oilfields of the 1930s having been shockingly low.

Papa looked just like Lyndon Johnson; he had the same malformed nose as Johnson, and the same squinty, mischievous eyes, and he even wore the same small, beige

Stetson. Mother claimed this resemblance was a curse from God, because Papa hated LBJ more than any other human, living or dead, for his support of school integration and civil rights. Papa hated Lyndon Johnson even more than he hated Martin Luther King, since Johnson had, to my grandfather's mind, betrayed his state and spoiled his Party. Even in the mid-1990s, twenty years or more after Johnson's death, Papa often complained, "Why, I'd love to dig up LBJ and sock him." Though a loyal Dixiecrat through the 1964 election, Papa became what Mother called a Mad Dog Republican afterward, although he did support the segregationist George Wallace when he ran for president in 1968 as the American Independent Party candidate.

For years, Nana and Papa kept an old billboard up in the pasture next to the freeway which read GEORGE WALLACE IN '68. Mother hated Papa's George Wallace sign, and not just because she felt it made the two of us, while sleeping soundly in our South Will Rise Again house, potential targets of racial violence. According to Papa, black people had tried to burn it down three times in the middle of the night, but he kept tacking it back up again, and replacing all the charred wood. Mother hated Nana and Papa's politics; her own family of Dixiecrats, the Wilsons, had remained forever loyal to the Democratic Party.

By 1996, even the small details of Daddy's family's life infuriated her. Mother hated it that Edie and Ida were mindless women who spent their days talking about soap opera characters as if they were real people, and making foods out of other foods. She hated it that Nana was fat, and wouldn't wear a girdle with a silk dress. Mother hated the fact that my grandmother videotaped old reruns of *The Lawrence Welk Show* and went to sleep every night with a heavy dose of Nyquil, and Mr. Welk's stars, the Semonski Sisters and Peanuts Hucko, serenading her. Mother hated Linda, Nana's Jehovah's Witness housekeeper. Mother and I called Linda "Fluffy," because she sometimes wore a sweatshirt that read I'M NOT FAT, I'M JUST FLUFFY. "Everybody else in the world slams the door when the Jehovah's Witnesses come knocking," Mother complained. "But not your Nana. She hires Fluffy to come clean her house five days a week."

Nana and Fluffy had planned that spring evening of 1996, when Mother had hated my grandmother so loudly, to be a celebration: Fluffy had recently chanced upon the secret of making biscuits out of boxed pancake batter, and Nana talked about this as if she and Fluffy had made some great scientific discovery. That evening, biscuits covered a conspicuous amount of table space, and Mother and I sensed some enormous expectation that we should eat one. This had caused us to abstain in protest, but Nana looked so pitiful that in the end Mother gave up and reached for one.

As soon as Mother took her first bite of biscuit, Nana leaned in across the dinner table. "Jessica," she said, "would you say that there is anything unusual about that biscuit you're eatin'?"

"No, Dot," Mother said. "I wouldn't say there's anything unusual about the biscuit." Nana's name had been, once, Dorothy. But she'd been a grandmother for so long, and she looked so old, that every other living human called her "Nana," except Mother.

"Does it taste . . ." Nana paused. "Does it taste, would you say, fresh?"

"Yes."

"Would you describe it as being a light and airy biscuit?"

"Yes. Light and airy."

"Doesn't taste mealy, or tough, or anything like that?"

"No."

"Well, what would you say . . . what would you have to say to me if I were to tell you that that biscuit you've been eating, the very biscuit that you say tastes so fresh, like it was baked in nature almost . . . is made from boxed pancake batter!"

"Jesus Christ, Dot," Mother moaned. "You'd think you'd split the fucking atom. It's a goddamned biscuit for fuck's sake."

For a moment, it looked as though Nana was succumbing to an apoplectic fit. The wattles under her neck trembled. Little purple veins appeared at her temples, and I was afraid she'd choke on her tongue. "Have you just completely lost your mind," Nana asked, "talking to me with that kind of vulgar language?"

"Oh, Dot," Mother said. "I think I must have lost my mind a long time ago."

Mother stood up and straightened her skirt. She tossed one of Mrs. Florenzo's Irish linen napkins down on her plate of half-eaten biscuit and slammed the screen door behind her as she left Nana and Papa's house.

I followed Mother out the screen door and heard Nana say, "Well, there goes a crazy woman if I've ever seen one." As it turned out, that evening was the last time Mother ever saw Nana, and the last time I would see her for many years, even though we would continue to live just across the pasture for nearly a year.

For a long time, Mother made up little prayers and songs about how much she wished Nana and Papa and Daddy would die so that she could inherit their money and move to Houston. I think Mother felt provoked by the near-supernatural immunity to illness that generations of desperate poverty seemed to have bred into the O'Dooles. Papa prided himself on his Irish toughness—to the O'Dooles, allergies were Yankee affectations. Papa and Daddy could clear patches of poison ivy with their bare hands without suffering a reaction. As far back as anyone could remember, no O'Doole had died before ninety, and except for applications of Nana's black salve, no one in Daddy's family ever seemed to require medical treatment. So in the face of the O'Dooles' resilience, Mother figured she had to resort to the hope of divine intervention because, according to her moral creed, divorce and murder were sins, but wishing and praying to Jesus that your in-laws would die was a spiritual exercise.

The most perfect of Mother's I Wish You Would Die songs was simple and catchy, and was, in fact, called "It Would Be So Great If You'd Just Die." (Imagine Irving Berlin alone at a piano.)

It would be so great if you'd just die.
Think of all the things that I could buy.
I could cash that check
If you'd just break your neck.
It would be so great if you'd just die.

(This song had many verses, but I'll skip to the big finale.)

Life would be so merry.
So, have a coronary.
You, I'd gladly bury,
So how 'bout hari-kari?
I'll call the mortuary.
It would be so great if you'd just die.

I found it upsetting when Mother sang me songs like this, but she said she had to because it was awful to write songs that were as good as hers that you couldn't sing to anybody because they'd think you were a bad person. Sometimes Mother would ask me to help her work out lyric schemes she was having trouble with. We'd be sitting at the kitchen table or on the sofa watching a movie, and she'd turn to me. She'd put down the newspaper, or mute the television set, and with a little *Eureka!* expression on her face, say something like "Quick. Help me think of all the words that rhyme with aneurism." I was, however, reasonably confident that Mother wasn't going to try to murder Daddy and Nana and Papa. I was reasonably certain of this because Mother insisted there was really no good way to kill somebody that wasn't obvious, like stabbing them or running them down with your car, where you didn't run the risk of them not dying, but just ending up an invalid you had to take care of for the rest of your life. "If I tried to, say, slowly poison your father, who's to say he wouldn't just end up a vegetable? Then I'd never get loose from him."

It was typical of the women in Mother's family to want to murder their husbands. According to Mother, it's very likely that her great-aunt Hazel actually did, while on vacation in Mexico, with a poisoned pina colada. Hazel had Uncle Hoke cremated in Acapulco, and when she returned to Houston, she had new calling cards printed up that read HAZEL PEACOCK FOX, WIDOW. Hazel was known among the women in Mother's family as the lucky one, both because her husband had died and because, when he did, he was very rich. Mother's women wanted money, and their fortunes seemed to be traveling the road opposite that of the O'Dooles'. "Here's how I see it, Robert. I'm miserable, yes. But I'd be more miserable if I were poor. I could divorce your father and have nothing. Or I can keep hoping for it all; that your grandparents will die, and I'll get everything. We'll just have to keep praying for a miracle, I guess."

Mother prayed for miracles, but in the meantime, she rented lots of movies. Mother loved the movies like a woman who believed in the fixed life of stories; in the inability of a movie to change itself no matter how many times you watched it, even if you finally ruined it by watching it so many times; who believed that her life was also a fixed story that couldn't change no matter what. She'd keep the same movie first in her Betamax, later in her VCR, until the tape was worn to tatters. Until she could play all the parts; until she could recite all the lines by heart, like a preacher can quote chapter and verse, or a classics scholar can quote the Fates of the *Oresteia*. Until it was terrifying. Until, when I said to her, "Hey, remember when Audrey Hepburn said to George Peppard in *Breakfast at Tiffany's*, 'I'm *maaaad* about Tiffany's.'" And Mother would say, as though defending something precious, "What she said, Robert . . . What Audrey Hepburn said to George Peppard was, 'I'm *craaaazy* about Tiffany's.' *Craaaazy*, Robert. Not *maaaad. Craaaazy*."

"Yes," I said. "Quite."

CHAPTER FOUR

French Leave

Though devastated by the discovery that Daddy had left her for another woman, Mother was relieved that Pam was both older and uglier than she, and so obviously so on both counts as to make common the opinion that my father had just completely lost his mind. That he was in the throes of a midlife crisis, and that even his midlife crisis was somehow terribly misfiring. Because to look at Mother and Pam was to receive the impression that the two—the wife and the mistress—had been somehow miscast, unaccountably assigned the other's part. Pam was a jockey and a groom at the racetrack, and a dirt clung beneath the short nails of her olive-colored hands that smelled of the stables. She was homely and brunette and mannish. And when I first met her, years later, I could only believe that Daddy had gone looking for an ordinary life, but had far overshot his intention and landed smack on top of drab Pam.

After Daddy brought Something New, brought Pam Who Smelled of the Stables, by my mother's house, I made some phone calls to a cousin in whom my father confided and found out where Pam lived, and where my father was now living. Even as I drove past it in the middle of the night, Pam's trailer house looked lopsided. Propped up on crumbly cinder blocks, it had bulging Coke-bottle-green plastic windows and appeared to be so light and shifty that even the halfhearted efforts of a disinterested Chevette could have overtaken it, could have hitched it up and hauled it off against its will. And it occurred to me, driving back to our big, white house on his parents' land, that in order to have been willing to move into that trailer, Daddy must have been pretty desperate to leave us.

Despite the fact that Pam was ugly, knowing that Daddy had left her for another woman catapulted Mother into a frenzy of beauty treatments, aerobic exercise, and various self-improvement measures. She quickly became convinced that her only hope of regaining financial comfort depended upon snaring a rich man before our new poverty began to appear too desperate and obvious. Even though Mother seemed a little berserk, I was grateful for her burst of new energy. It was far preferable to the way she'd moped around the house after seeing Pam wait for Daddy in our front hall.

After she saw Pam's poochy stomach, Mother had abandoned herself to *Breakfast at Tiffany's*. She spent days in her big canopy bed, wearing a dirty peignoir, watching her movie, and drinking vodka out of Evian bottles. *Breakfast at Tiffany's* had carried Mother through years of depression, and I knew to steer clear whenever I heard "Moon River" blaring out from underneath her bedroom door. And while I could often hear a woman crying, I couldn't be certain if that woman was Mother or Audrey Hepburn.

When Mother finally did get out of bed, she went straight to Neiman's and had Eduardo dye all of her wigs jet black "for a change."

"Jesus Christ," Mother sobbed into her mirror that night. "I was trying to look like *Elizabeth Taylor*. And this old man in the parking garage said I looked just like *Ann Miller*. You shoot for Liz Taylor and you get Ann Miller. Where's the fucking humanity?!" The next day Mother went back to blonde, and asked if I thought she needed a face-lift. "Oh, I feel old, Robert. I feel like a forgotten woman. I feel like Joanne Carson. I feel like Sybil Burton. My god," Mother gasped, *"I feel like Dore Previn."*

I'd felt Mother was safe, somehow, as long as she kept watching *Breakfast at Tiffany's*. But then, one night, something really troubling occurred. I couldn't sleep from worrying about money and worrying about where Mother and I would live after her divorce was finalized. Between my cold sweats and the hot, soupy air of the Texas June night, the sheets on my bed were wet and heavy. I'd spent hours trying to hypnotize myself by staring deep into the ceiling fan slowly turning above my bed. When that hadn't worked, I finally got up and wandered down to the kitchen to get a Coca-Cola—where the sight of Mother sitting in the dark startled me.

"Good God, what are you doing sitting in the dark? I thought you were upstairs watching your movie."

"I'm sick to death of that movie. If I ever have to look at Audrey Hepburn's bony little face again, I'm going to puke all over myself."

When Mother got sick of *Breakfast at Tiffany's*, I became frightened for her for the first time since Daddy left. This was strange behavior for Mother. "When did this happen?" I asked.

"It happened in the middle of the part where Buddy Ebsen comes to New York to bring Holly back to Texas. I hate Buddy Ebsen. I started thinking about how much I hate Buddy Ebsen, and then I started thinking about how much I hate *The Beverly Hillbillies*, and then I suddenly realized that I hate *Breakfast at Tiffany's*."

"But you loved that movie," I said, fairly confident that I was hearing the first warning bell of Mother's full-on nervous breakdown.

"Well, now I hate it." Mother cracked her knuckles, and went back upstairs to bed.

At some point in the next few days, Mother replaced *Breakfast at Tiffany's* with *How to Marry a Millionaire*, a movie about three penniless Manhattan models who fake wealth in order to snare rich men. As terrified as I was by this new development, it proved to be the beginning of Mother's comeback. *How to Marry a Millionaire* reinvigorated Mother. In an early scene, Lauren Bacall lays a man trap: "We're going on a bear hunt, girls. The beautiful thing about a bear hunt is that all you've got to do is catch *one* big bear." Soon, Mother began repeating The Bear Hunt line while sitting at her vanity table blending lipstick colors together with a little mink brush, or doing the Jane Fonda workout video on the floor in front of her canopy bed.

I was grateful that Mother had managed to be reinvigorated by something, even if it was only some dialogue from an old movie. She needed to harness all of her inner strength in order to address our troubling financial situation. It hadn't taken us long to run out of money and max out all of Mother's charge cards. And we'd just begun looting the house for returnable items we could exchange at department stores for cash or necessities—a lightly worn cashmere suit was, for instance, exchanged at Saks for half a month's worth of lunches in their third-floor café. But this could serve as our source of income for only so long, and Mother knew it. So every time a pair of Ferragamo pumps went back to the department store, Mother's manhunt got a little more serious.

I, of course, found it sad that Mother's ambition was to use beauty makeovers to fool some rich man into marrying her, but it also offended my political sensibilities. I considered myself a feminist—the only feminist at Trinity Lutheran High School. I'd found the old *Norton Anthology* Mother used for her American literature courses at Texas A&M and had fallen in love with the poetry of Anne Sexton and Adrienne Rich. And every day, Gloria Steinem's quip that most women in America lived one man away from welfare took on an increasingly personal meaning for me. Mother considered herself to be a feminist, too. She thought if you tricked a man, that made you a feminist. She also really liked the way Gloria Steinem did her eyelashes.

"Mother, I think you need to consider that you're terrified of aging, and that you're desperate for the approval of The Masculine Gaze."

"Nope. What I'm terrified of is poverty, Robert. And what I'm desperate for is some money."

"What about becoming a career woman?" I asked.

"Going to work just *ruins* the whole day."

"So what about graduate school?" I asked.

"Please," Mother said.

"I just think you might want to use this opportunity to discover something about yourself, that's all."

"Don't worry about me, Robert. Besides, I kind of feel like I *am* discovering myself—a lot of women do, you know, after their husbands take French Leave. What I keep trying to remember is that Wallis Simpson didn't marry Edward VIII until she was forty-five. Who knows, maybe my prince will come any day now."

Two months later, Mother was back on birth control pills, juggling the affections of her born-again Christian divorce lawyer and a toupéed man named Taft who owned a vast chain of twenty-four-hour roadside breakfast joints across West Texas. Of the two, I preferred Mr. Taft, even though his fake hair caused him to have an inordinate fear of stiff breezes. He was the only person I've ever known who licked his index finger and pointed it out the window to gauge the strength of the wind. Even so, he was worlds better boyfriend material than Mother's divorce lawyer— a wild-eyed religious fanatic with a long Jeremiah's beard who belonged to a near cult of Houston businessmen who saw Jesus in terms of their own corporate savvy. "When you really think about it," he once told me, "Jesus was the great litigator of his time."

Mother's lawyer-boyfriend had a knack for grafting the ambitions of this world onto visions of the next, and I worried that his skills as an attorney might suffer from the strength of his faith. One afternoon, Mother succumbed to tears in his long-windowed office, trying to describe just how urgent our financial situation had become. "Don't worry, Jessica," he consoled her. "The year 2000's not far off. It won't be long now 'til the rapture comes."

Mother's dating had adopted a frantic pace because we were high-and-dry broke, and we'd finally exhausted returnable clothing as a source of income. In fact, by early August we were largely living off the daily shipments of brioche and jelly rolls that Mr. Taft made fresh in his restaurant chain and air-mailed to Mother from Lubbock as courting gifts. "There's something revolting about a man," Mother said, "who views pastry as seduction."

Even though Mother had a profound faith in Jesus, and was a great advocate of the power of prayer to smite bad drivers and tacky in-laws, she'd never been a regular churchgoer. We were, officially, Southern Baptists, but that was really just a social convenience. However, in the weeks after Daddy left, she'd started cruising Bible study groups at Houston's more affluent Protestant churches. And her eyes had begun to shine like a jungle cat's with a renewed social ambition unseen since her college campaign for Cotton Bowl princess. In no time, she'd laid bear traps in houses of Christian worship throughout the greater Houston metropolitan area, joining several Republican luncheon clubs along the way.

"But you're a registered Democrat," I objected. "Nobody in your family's voted Republican since Appomattox Courthouse."

"From now on, Robert," Mother told me, "I vote with the Democrats and lunch with the Republicans."

Mother had started making friends with women again, in order to aid in her manhunt. Her divorce lawyer-boyfriend had been located through her new best girlfriend, Eddie—whom she'd met in the buffet line of a breakfast prayer meeting she'd shown up late to, in a Baptist church the size of the Astrodome in one of Houston's wealthier neighborhoods. Eddie was a mean old lady with orange, pointy hair that looked like a traffic cone, who bore a striking resemblance to Endora, the Agnes Moorehead character on *Bewitched*. She was completely friendless and willing to introduce Mother to her congregation's stock of marriageable professionals. Among them, Mother's new, apocalyptic divorce lawyer.

Since man-hunting seemed to be the only bond of their friendship, Eddie struck me as a bad influence on Mother. After they took to sharing clothes, fey polka-dotted dresses began turning up in Mother's closet. "What a man wants is a girl on his arm," I heard Eddie say to Mother one Sunday in the church parking lot. Eddie idled her old Mercedes next to Mother's Jaguar in order to lend her some dresses she'd brought from home. The dresses were crammed so tightly into a single plastic dry-cleaner's bag that they looked like a wad of laminated silk patterns. And though it was hard to tell where one dress ended and another began, I got the sinking feeling that each of the dresses was, somehow, ruffled.

"I think these little dresses are gonna suit you to a tee, sugar," Eddie told Mother. "If I were you, I might think about steering towards the springtime colors. And, by the way," she said, before slowly coasting her Mercedes out of the lot, "if you ever want the number of a good doctor who can tighten that jaw right up for you, you'll let me know, won't you, honey pie?"

"I hate that old lady's guts," I said to Mother.

"Well, I don't like her much myself, but she knows *everybody* at church. And she's made me do some hard thinking about how preferable widowers are to divorcés, in addition to explaining the folly of my thinking of a search for a new husband as a bear hunt. Eddie insists men are nothing *at all* like bears. Men, Eddie says, are like dogs. Now, a widower is a good, housebroken creature that's been trained not to piss all over your home and chase after pussycats. But a divorced man's like a dog you find at the pound. He might swear up and down that he's purebred, and that he's only up for adoption through freak circumstances. But you'll never really know what landed him in the pound 'til you've signed the papers and taken him home. And by that time, you're just stuck."

"But, Mother," I said, "just because a man's wife *dies* doesn't mean he's been a good husband to her. Besides, I don't like the way Eddie talks about your looks. Just be yourself, and I'm sure you'll find a boyfriend."

"I don't want a boyfriend, Robert. What I want is a rich husband. And it wouldn't hurt me to spruce myself up a little bit. Eddie's right. What the men want is young, young, young."

It seemed that, overnight, Mother's makeup took on a certain Maytime glow. Her wigs grew longer and blonder, and once, I swear, I saw her sporting a ponytail. Suddenly, all of her dresses were ruffled, as though her wardrobe had been infected by Eddie's single, contaminated drycleaner's bag.

All in all, the illusion didn't hold, as Mother started to resemble those flashback sequences in the movies, in which an older actress—Shirley MacLaine, for instance—is made up to look like a younger version of herself, and ends up, instead, just looking like an older woman *made up to look like* a younger version of herself.

I made a point of telling Mother that I felt men appreciated a womanly beauty. And I scissored some pictures of Catherine Deneuve and Jeanne Moreau out of *Paris Match*, and left them on Mother's nightstand, trying to give her examples of women whose looks had mellowed and gotten finer with age. But even as I did, I knew it was pointless.

"I want to look *younger*," Mother told me.

"Than *what*?" I asked.

CHAPTER FIVE

The Lady Vanishes

In the early hours of a late-August morning, two weeks before I began my junior year at Trinity and a month before my seventeenth birthday, Mother shook me awake by the shoulders. For three days she'd complained of a pain in her abdomen, and a feared overdose of birth control pills. These complaints had escalated in alarm as, throughout the night, Mother began to bleed heavily from her feminine parts. "Robert, get up," she yelled. "You've got to get me to the hospital. My *thing's* still bleeding. I need you to drive me into Houston. I called the doctor's office; they're expecting us any minute."

I threw on stray clothes and rushed downstairs. Mother had the car waiting, with her overnight case packed and stashed into the backseat. And though I was afraid I wouldn't get Mother to the doctor's office in time, and afraid she'd bleed to death in the passenger's seat, it was the sight of her overnight case that frightened me the most. It suggested Mother believed her condition to be serious, and that her stay in the hospital might be a long one.

The road was still dark as we drove away from Petunia, but corners of the sky were already streaked with bright, wet patches of pastel light. And though the dim Interstate was beginning to fill with people heading for work, I was able to keep the car going almost eighty by veering wildly through traffic, the hazard lights of Mother's Jaguar blinking fire. At sixteen, this was the first time I'd driven recklessly for the sake of emergency. I all but hoped we'd be pulled over, so that I could scold the offending traffic cop and commandeer him as our escort.

Mother held her stomach and moaned and clutched her armrest, saying things like "Oh, the pain. My god, the pain." And "I sure do hope we make it in time, Robert. Jesus, please let us make it in time." I wrote off Mother's wooden speech to pain and slight delirium, and responded in kind with "We will, Mother, we will. Rest now, and listen to the radio." But even as I said it, and dawn slowly rose beyond the crowding Houston freeway, the idea did occur to me that our situation seemed less like illness than like illness in the movies.

Once, when I was in the second grade, I'd tried to see how far I could walk blindfolded in an absolutely straight line, using the barbed wire fence in Papa's back pasture as my gauge. I'd made it almost ten feet before feeling a small prick against my neck, and opening my eyes, I realized I'd turned, and walked into the barbed wire. Because I wasn't in pain, I couldn't quite recognize the bright red smear on my white shirt, until I touched my fingers to my neck to see if I might be the source of it. As I drew my hand away, it too was covered in blood. Color spots flashed and twinkled about my head as I ran to my father, mending the same barbed wire fence about a hundred yards away. Seeing me, Daddy made a hysterical gulping sound, something between a hiccup and a laugh, then took off my T-shirt and tied it around my neck to slow the bleeding. After scooping me into his pickup, he sped me to the emergency room, where it turned out my cut wasn't very serious, though it could have been. I'd come within centimeters of puncturing my jugular vein.

What I remember most about this experience was not being able to believe that what was happening to me was real—I never felt any pain, and I wasn't particularly frightened—not until it was all over, and I realized how close I'd come to being badly hurt. I remember Daddy gunning the engine of his truck, frantic to get me to the doctor, and being surprised I wasn't more upset. It seemed like everything—Daddy's fear, and the gravel and dirt flying from the bumpy roads leading off the ranch, even the blood on my T-shirt—was harmless, and like it was gliding past.

Now, driving Mother to the Houston Medical Center, I was the frantic one. But even still, I felt a certain failure to connect what was happening to reality. Mother pointed me toward Skylark Towers—a complex of offices connected to the Methodist hospital through a series of long, white underground tunnels, telling me her doctor was on its twelfth floor. "Valet-park," Mother instructed.

"You really *are* sick," I said. Only neither of us felt like laughing as I pulled into a hedge-trimmed carport, where a Puerto Rican valet took the keys and gave me a claim ticket, and Mother jumped from the car and ran into the building. She stood holding an elevator in the gray marble lobby. By the time I cleared the elevator's sliding doors it was just past eight o'clock, but the hospital still seemed drowsy, and a smattering of nurses with black-rimmed eyes shuffled across the lobby wearing green scrubs.

As soon as we reached the twelfth floor, Mother hurried me toward the only office that seemed open. A television was tuned to the *Today Show* in a small room with salmon-colored vinyl love seats. Al Roker was giving the weather forecast. We were the office's first patients of the morning. Mother began speaking frantically to a woman behind a fogged, sliding-glass partition, who handed her a clipboard, and asked her to sign the register.

I sat down and tried to distract myself from Mother's pacing across the linoleum floor by concentrating on the weather report—something about record temperatures and midwestern farmers—but I couldn't focus my attention. Mother's high heels made the tile floor sound hollow until she suddenly stopped pacing and turned to me: "I have *got* to go to the bathroom, Robert," Mother said. "I've got to go to the bathroom real bad. I'll be right back." Mother grabbed her purse and overnight case, and rushed out the office door to the ladies' room down the hall.

"Should I follow you, Mother?" I called after her. "Do you want me to wait outside the door? Just in case?"

But Mother had already rounded the corner. So I returned to the office to wait, on the off chance that while

Mother was gone, her name might be called. And a few minutes later, it was—by an ash-blond nurse in a too-tight uniform. "Jessica Wilson," she called.

I took the nurse's hair color as a bad sign. For years, Mother had shared with me her grandmother Eugenia's wisdom about The Ways of the World: "Never dance with a man with a pencil mustache, Jessica," Eugenia had warned Mother as a little girl. "And always beware of ash blondes."

"Why?" I'd often asked Mother. "What's wrong with ash blondes?"

But Mother had just shaken her head and stared into the distance, as though the truth were too terrible to speak.

There were moments when I suspected that Eugenia's advice to Mother had not been entirely grounded in common sense. However. This particular ash blonde did indeed seem like someone to be wary of—she looked cranky, and her uniform kept riding up on her. "She's in the ladies' room," I said to the nurse. "She'll be right back. I'm her son."

"She a new patient?" asked the nurse.

"I'm pretty sure she's not," I said.

"Well, we don't seem to have no record of her. Or of her appointment, neither." There seemed to be some bacon wedged between the nurse's front teeth.

"Well, that sounds like a mistake to me," I said, remembering that Mother had come unhesitatingly to this office, having called in advance. "My mother spoke with someone from your office on the telephone early this morning. The doctor should be expecting her."

"Yeah? What seems to be the problem with your mama?" the ash blonde asked. Her head was slowly tilting backward, until she stared at me over her nose.

"My mother is hemorrhaging," I said. "This is an emergency." My voice cracked in concern. "And since she's been in the ladies' room quite some time now, I think *somebody* ought to go check on her." I eyed the ash blonde in such a way as to make obvious that that somebody was her.

The nurse grunted and headed reluctantly down the hall, her hips lazily shifting. She returned before the door seemed to fully rest in its frame. "There ain't nobody in that bathroom," she said.

I pushed past her in a cold sweat and ran to check the ladies' room myself.

It was, indeed, empty. Though I could have sworn I caught a faint hint of Mother's perfume.

Rushing from the bathroom, I fully expected to find Mother collapsed somewhere on the hallway's industrial carpeting. A fluorescent light flickered and buzzed as I walked slowly back to the doctor's office. It was still early in the morning. I didn't yet feel fully awake, and it crossed my mind that I could be making some awful, groggy mistake. "I just don't understand," I said to the ash blonde nurse leaning in the doorway. "Is there another ladies' room on this floor? Could she have met some other nurse in the hallway who's already taken her into the examination room? Is there a different entrance to this office?"

"There's only one way to get into this office, and that's walking right through this door. And you're looking at all the nurses this office's got."

"So there's no one else who works here? You were the person Mother talked to on the telephone this morning?"

"I said I'm the only *nurse*. I don't answer phones. That's what the receptionist gets paid for."

"Then I want to speak to the receptionist," I said. My voice sounded thin and wispy, like it was made of smoke.

"Fine," she said. "Wait here." Like she was grateful for any chance to shake loose of me.

The nurse was gone a long while, and I could barely hear someone talking behind the glass partition. On TV, two English ladies were showing Katie Couric how to make cucumber salad. And when the nurse finally returned, the receptionist, a pillowy woman in a faded silk jacket, followed her. "Son," said the receptionist. She sat down beside me and put her hand on my knee. I crossed my legs in order to take her hand *off* my knee. "I hear you're havin' some trouble finding your mama." As though I were a toddler found wandering a shopping mall.

"My mother," I said, "is hemorrhaging from her feminine parts." I leaned forward, attempting to impart the urgency of our situation. "She must be a regular patient of yours because she called you before coming here. I'm absolutely terrified she's collapsed somewhere in your facility, and I think it's your responsibility to send somebody [I briefly glanced at the ash-blond nurse] out looking for her." I tried to imagine myself testifying in open court regarding the lack of professional concern I'd confronted in this office, hoping some small trace of this thought colored my tone.

"But, hon," the receptionist said, like she wasn't sure whether to be frightened of or for me, "this is a *podiatrist's* office. What I don't understand is why your mama would come see us when her pretty's bleeding. Unless. Nothing's gone wrong with her feet, too, has there?"

The ash blonde chortled.

I shook my head to clear my ears. The whole morning had rushed by me, but now I had the experience of time grinding still. My stomach felt like that machine that stretches salt-water taffy at the rodeo. I felt like anything I might say to this woman would sound totally insane. Like that moment in *The Lady Vanishes* when the hero keeps insisting that there *really* had been an old lady on the train, and she really was kidnapped—but the more he keeps insisting, the crazier he sounds.

I stood up and walked to the door. An etched plastic plaque identified the office as belonging to Dr. Stanley Bartlestein, DPM. Which I'd noticed before, but hadn't read, and even if I had, I wouldn't have known that DPM meant Doctor of Podiatry.

I walked slowly back to the salmon vinyl love-seat. I must have seemed too prissy to be a lunatic or prankster. Seeing how deeply she'd chilled me, the pillowy receptionist once again placed her hand on my knee, except this time I didn't brush it away. "Honey, if you'd like, you can come around to the office, and I'll check for her name in the computer one more time."

"I guess so," I said. It wasn't much of an offer, but it was the best I was likely to receive.

I followed her behind the sliding-glass partition, to her desk, where she offered me a seat in a swivel-chair and typed mother's name into the computer. And retrieved nothing.

"Would you mind trying her married name?" I asked, remembering that since Daddy left us, Mother's surname had fluctuated with her moods.

"Jessica O'Doole" also retrieved nothing. The computer gazed back at me, unblinking.

"I just don't understand," I muttered again, now *feeling* like a toddler deserted in a shopping mall. "Would you mind if I just sat in your reception room for a little while . . ." I managed to say before my voice trailed off. Because at that moment, I didn't truly believe I would ever see my mother again. I hadn't seen Daddy since he'd disappeared from my life a couple of months earlier, and it crossed my mind that it was within the realm of human possibility that Mother could disappear, too. That she might have just chosen some random podiatrist's office to leave me in forever, after stringing me along with some loopy story about her vagina.

I mean, *sure*, now that I thought about it, it didn't seem likely that taking too many birth control pills could result in a vaginal hemorrhage. And even if it did, Petunia's local emergency room would probably have been a wiser place to seek medical treatment than a downtown doctor's office. But Mother had acted with such direction, and I'd gotten up *so early*, that it hadn't occurred to me to question her story until now. Which was a fact that offered little reassurance regarding my future performance on the SATs— although in my defense, and though Mother and I often pushed the conventional boundaries of the mother-son relationship, I did not, even under peculiar circumstances, wish to delve too closely into Mother's vagina. Which was, I concluded, exactly what made it a ripe field for deception.

But realizing this brought me no closer to an explanation of what I was really doing in Dr. Bartlestein's office. I still had Mother's valet-parking ticket, though I supposed it was possible to retrieve a car without it. But the fact that she'd let me keep it in the first place suggested to me that Mother must have intended to come back. And that, whatever was going on, there must have been some reason she'd wanted me to remain at Dr. Bartlestein's. Mother had been pretty frenzied lately, about money and remarriage. But I still thought she was functioning as a fairly rational human being. Since I didn't have anybody to call and ask for advice, and I was far away from home, I decided to check and see if Mother's car was still parked downstairs. If it was, I'd return to Dr. Bartlestein's, and wait on one of his vinyl love-seats until Mother came for me, or until the ash-blonde nurse kicked me out, whichever came first.

Throughout the morning, and then the afternoon, the receptionist, whose name, I learned, was Gladys, plied me with peppermints from a green glass bowl and Dr. Peppers so cold from the specimen freezer they were tissued with ice. Gladys told me to make myself comfortable in front of the TV—and between shows, I made odd dashes downstairs, to check with the car-park, and make certain Mother's Jaguar was still in the lot, afraid that the moment I left Dr. Bartlestein's office would be the moment

Mother chose to return. Each time, the car was just as we'd left it that morning.

A fat police officer patrolled the hospital's entry on a golf cart, and every time he puttered by, I thought about asking for help. But I felt pathetic enough already, and while, thanks to Gladys's sympathy, I was being allowed to quietly wait out the day at Dr. Bartlestein's, I knew if I involved anyone else, I'd end up trying to explain my mother to one stranger after another, which was a thought that made me miserable. So mostly, I watched TV and allowed myself to be soothed by Gladys's Dr. Peppers, filling out *Cosmo* quizzes as hobbling fleets of old ladies stumbled through the day complaining of bunions and trading folk therapies for ingrown toenails. I felt strangely in context. It's pretty hard to get kicked out of a hospital. As an institution, it's used to its odd stragglers; people who're intent on waiting forever if they're put to it, and others who aren't sure when to give up and go home. The cracks in the vinyl seat pinched me, and pulled the hair on the back of my legs. I waited there for hours.

I waited in Dr. Stanley Bartlestein's office from Katie Couric through Oprah Winfrey, until I felt crazy for waiting; and until I started to believe that my earlier suspicion, when Mother had suddenly stopped watching *Breakfast at Tiffany's,* had been correct, and that she *was* having a nervous breakdown. Or that she'd run off with some Republican surgeon she'd met at the Baptist church, and that Skylark Towers was just a convenient rendezvous point for their elopement to Mexico, and that maybe Mother had left me her Jaguar as an apology. If this last alternative was what had really happened, I decided, it was, all in all, a reality I could live with.

Then, halfway through *Oprah*, at almost three-thirty, Gladys waved me towards the sliding-glass window, to tell me she'd received a phone call from someone who'd instructed me to report to an office on the third floor, number 305. "Good luck, hon," Gladys said, seeming in equal measures curious and embarrassed for me. I felt dazed by the events of the day. It was another of those moments when everything seemed unreal. I proceeded to the elevator.

The door to office number 305 was unmarked, except for a shining brass crucifix nailed into its linoleum paneling.

And as soon as I saw that crucifix, I knew exactly where I was. *This* was a plastic surgeon's office. An Evangelical plastic surgeon's office.

The lights in the office were elegantly dimmed, and the walls were covered with pictures of women with faces like well-made beds and Jesus holding hands with the little children. The mauve carpet was so thick it felt like you were walking on the moon. As I walked toward the receptionist's kidney-shaped desk, the door to an examination room swung confidentially shut on a swollen, bandaged body that I recognized as my mother. Eddie, Mother's new church girlfriend, sat cross-legged in a black leather chair. I hadn't seen Eddie at first on account of the room being so elegantly dimmed. She batted cigarette ashes into an empty Coca-Cola can, and looked at the receptionist, and pointed her cigarette at me.

I started to introduce myself to the receptionist, whose

face was stiff and waxy, but Eddie interrupted me: "Please have your mother's car parked at the hospital's side entrance, and make sure the top's raised."

"I'm afraid I'm not quite crystal on what's going on here," I said.

Eddie looked slowly up at me from the Coca-Cola can and handed me a parking validation form in a talon of pink, opalescent fingernail polish. The age freckles on her hand looked like leopard spots. Eddie hadn't liked me from the start of her friendship with Mother, because she saw herself as Mother's Indian guide in the hunt for a new husband. In this capacity, she'd encouraged Mother to appear as young and girlish as possible. Eddie had made it clear that being seen around church with a sixteen-year-old son aged a woman in the congregation's eyes. "Every time you bring your son to church," she told Mother, "you just ruin your chances of marrying a good Christian man." So far, this wasn't a piece of Eddie's advice that Mother had heeded, and this irritated Eddie.

The other reason Eddie didn't care for me was because she hated "the homos," and from the beginning, she'd had her suspicions about me. "That son of yours seems a little funny," Eddie told Mother one day after I'd dropped Mother off at Eddie's condo, wearing a T-shirt with a picture of Joan Crawford from *Strait-Jacket* and a caption that read DON'T FUCK WITH ME, BOYS. THIS AIN'T MY FIRST TIME AT THE RODEO!

Eddie stared at me flatly, like I was the bellboy come to collect her luggage. She waved the parking validation form at me with her hand, and said again slowly, "Have your mother's car parked at the hospital's side entrance, and make sure the top's raised." Like she was providing deep background. As though she were Carl Sagan explaining the long history of consciousness.

I looked at Eddie and tried to think of something really vicious to say, but I was so surprised to see her and so hurt by the fact that Mother had confided in her, and not me, that I couldn't think of anything *to* say. So I just stood there looking at Eddie with my head cocked and my mouth open. "My mother's absolutely fine?" I finally asked. "This whole production was about what, a face-lift?"

"*Of course not,*" Eddie said. "Do you think the doctor would send your mother home this quick after a face-lift? She got lip and breast implants."

"But she didn't need any of that," I said.

Eddie gathered her lips together like she was kissing the air. She exhaled a long puff of smoke and continued to hold the parking validation form out to me. "Oh, he's worried about his mommy, isn't he? Well, all you have to worry about is having the car parked. Think you can handle it?" Then she wagged the form at me one final time before I snatched it out of her spotted hand, and left.

I left the elegantly dark, Baptist plastic surgeon's office with Eddie's parking validation form, took the elevator down to the hospital's marble lobby, and requested that the valet, finally, bring Mother's car around to the hospital's side entrance. I requested that he leave the top raised. And when he did, I took the driver's seat, and waited.

The fat cop in the golf cart kept wheeling by the side door, barking at me about obstructing traffic and ordering me, at regular five-minute intervals, to circle the block. "If you wanna park, then you're gonna have to do it in the garage." He was eating a jelly doughnut from a waxed paper bag. Raspberry-flavored ooze smeared the gray stubble of his chin.

The cop made me circle the building three times, and just as he was about to demand that I make it a fourth, my mother was wheeled out in a chair by two male orderlies—Sophie Tucker flanked by white-tailed chorus boys. Eddie followed, shielding her eyes from the sun with her hand.

Mother wore a blue hospital sheath, and little wisps of hair floated off her head like dandelion fuzz. Her wig and clothes had been stuffed into her overnight case, which Eddie carried, along with Mother's purse. The orderlies placed Mother into the passenger seat, lifting her like a piece of delicate furniture. Then Eddie threw the overnight case into the popped trunk, shut it, and walked around to the passenger's-side door.

Eddie leaned into Mother, who was motionless in her seat, kissed her cheek, and reached her right arm over Mother's lap, buckling her seatbelt. I could smell Eddie's perfume—like a preservative, sharp like mothballs and musty. She looked over Mother's head and straight into my eyes. "Your *boy* here was so afraid that we'd done something bad to his mommy that . . ." But just then I toed the gas, and Eddie tumbled away from our car, kept from hurting herself by the catch of Mother's burly orderlies. Mother's door swung shut from the force of the car's momentum, and a silence lay between us as we drove away from Eddie and the orderlies, away from Jelly Doughnut and Dr. Bartlestein, and headed for the Interstate.

To the extent that her bulging lips and chest, her bruised and bandaged face would allow, Mother fluttered and undulated like Charo. She was obviously drugged and in pain, but even still, I could tell she was a little pleased at having got one over on me. She arched her eyebrows and blinked in a sort of feline way. She did everything but pat me on the shoulder with a painted fan and say, "My, my, I do declare."

"Mother," I said quietly, "I've been petrified for the past three days about your thing bleeding. Not just about whether or not my mother was going to be okay. But also, where we were going to get the money for a doctor. And whether or not the check to the insurance company bounced."

"Now, Robert, would you have rushed me to the hospital this early in the morning if you'd known it was only plastic surgery I was getting?" Mother said this in a tone of voice most typically reserved for "fiddle-dee-dee."

"So you just decided to tell me your vagina was bleeding? I mean, I'm not even going to ask where you got the money for this. I just . . . This was a terrible day for me, Mother. What you did to me today was really *awful*."

"Could we possibly postpone the conversation about what a horrible mother I am until a time when I'm not convalescing from surgery?"

"I'm working very hard," I said, "to decide whether or not you're having a nervous breakdown. Or if you've always been crazy, and I'm just now waking up to it."

"I am not crazy, Robert," Mother said. "What I am is

desperate. I've told you that before. Look at me. Don't I look like a desperate woman?"

I glanced at Mother, and was forced to admit that without her wig, dressed in a hospital gown, with the lower half of her face bruised over and a little trail of spittle trickling down from her swollen lips, she did sort of fit my mental picture of a desperate woman.

"You remember that movie, *I Want to Live!*?" Mother asked.

"Yes . . ."

"Remember when Susan Hayward says, 'Don't ya know what it's like to be desperate?' "

"Yeah. So what?"

"Well, now I know. Anyway, I have to rest my eyes now." Only, Mother didn't rest her eyes. She stared off beyond the Houston freeway system—her mind, doubtless, mapping the future.

CHAPTER SIX

Pig Fuck

"Well, hasn't your life just gone from quail eggs on toast to shit on a shovel?" asked my grandmother JoAnn when I phoned her during Mother's convalescence from her lip and breast implants. It was the first time I'd spoken to JoAnn in almost ten years—since Mother had cut off all contact with her mother after an ill-timed trip to Acapulco. In the two months since Daddy left, I'd suggested calling my grandmother a number of times, to ask for money. But Mother had always refused, insisting JoAnn would only be gratified by her suffering. "Your grandmother lacks the refinement of our bleeding-heart sensitivity, Robert," Mother said. "Besides, if I had to sit and listen to that old lady crow, I think I'd puke all over myself."

In the years since I'd seen her, JoAnn had gone to great efforts to remain part of my life—principally by having lavish presents, like a Vespa, or a sailboat, delivered to

Nana and Papa's ranch for my birthdays and Christmases. And while Mother warned me that the real purpose of JoAnn's gifts had been to outshine her own, I'd contended my Vespa conveyed genuine feeling.

So I knew that, except for Daddy, there was no one Mother would be more furious about my discussing her troubles with than *her* mother. But in the days after I'd driven her home from the born-again plastic surgeon's office, I'd reached a point where I was willing to sacrifice a bit of Mother's pride. In those days Mother relied upon my round-the-clock care and attention. She couldn't afford a nurse, much less the hospital rest her doctor had recommended, and had only managed to finance her implants in the first place by hocking Daddy's diamond engagement ring at a Petunia pawnshop called The Love It or Leave It— a discovery I made, finally, by withholding Mother's pain medication. And while I had no idea how JoAnn felt about her daughter, after not having spoken to her in almost a decade, I figured there was no one more qualified to advise me on Mother's strange behavior. And I felt certain my grandmother loved me and would, at the very least, send cash if I begged for it.

I admit it had been galling, at first, being forced to accept responsibility for Mother's convalescence. I *was* furious with her for lying to me about her plastic surgery. Under the circumstances, I'd resented sleeping on the chaise in Mother's bedroom—to be nearby in case she needed me in the middle of the night. Since Mother's chest hurt too much for her to get out of bed by herself, she even needed my help walking to the bathroom. Her lips were so swollen and tender that she could only sip room-temperature chicken broth through plastic straws. And though the preparation of her food hadn't amounted to much labor, I'd resented every crank of the can opener required to take the lids off her Campbell's soup cans. But Mother looked so pitiful, laid up in her canopy bed with the lower half of her face bruised black, it was impossible to hold a grudge for long.

Until the swelling of her lips went down, Mother spoke with a lisp. And while every word seemed bumbling and painful, her eyes shone when speaking of her new, improved dating potential: "Conthidering the men my new lipth will bring my way, Robert, I'll be shopping for new diamond ringth in no time." Even when heavy dosages of painkillers caused her to waft through hours in a semiconscious state, her eyelids fluttered from sweet dreams about diamonds and rich divorcés.

After paying for her plastic surgeries, Mother's jewelry case was almost bare—all she had left was a bracelet arranged so the diamonds and emeralds looked like daisies, and a few little silver rings and porcelain cameos that her grandmother Eugenia had left her when she died. Mother insisted she saw selling her jewelry merely as an investment in our future. But for me, the pawning of Mother's engagement ring was the final, tiny push I needed to fall across the border of Traumatized and into the land of the Hysterical—and to make me desperate enough to call my grandmother JoAnn. Maybe it was because Mother's engagement ring held her fattest, prettiest jewel: star-shaped and heavy looking, framed by a flurry of smaller stones in a neat platinum setting. Or maybe it was because the loss of Mother's ring symbolized, most clearly, the tawdry end of my parents' marriage. The hocking of a diamond engagement ring to pay for silicone implants seemed a pretty appropriate metaphor for my father abandoning Mother and me to move in with his pregnant girlfriend in her dilapidated mobile home.

But however tragic *I* found the loss of Mother's jewelry, JoAnn seemed strangely unmoved on that anxious afternoon when the vapor of chicken broth steamed the kitchen air and I broke down and called her, speaking softly, even after firmly convincing myself that Mother was reduced, by her noon dosage of painkillers, to a drooling stupor. "Hello, JoAnn," I said. (JoAnn had always insisted that I call her and Alfred by their first names: "After all, I'm a grandmother," she'd told me. "Not an old lady.") "It's me. Your grandson. Oh, JoAnn. It's been so long."

"Yes," JoAnn replied. "Hi."

Considering the sums JoAnn had laid out on my birthday presents over the years, I'd expected a certain enthusiasm when she recognized my voice, freshly deepened by puberty. I had also expected a fair amount of sympathy, and no small amount of shock, when I conveyed, in full, pathetic detail, the tailspin our life had taken. I told JoAnn that Mother and I had been abandoned by Daddy for a pregnant jockey. And that Mother had been forced to sell her diamonds to pay for the plastic surgery she hoped would help her snare a rich man. I told JoAnn that since we'd fired Juana, our housekeeper, I'd had to purchase two-dollar shirts from the five-and-dime that I threw away after wearing just once because all of my regular clothes smelled like sweat, I didn't know how to use the washing machine, and Mother said that laundry was the sort of dull, tedious chore that courted clinical depression. And, finally, I confessed to my grandmother that our finances had reached such a low ebb that Mother and I were reduced to doing poor people things like getting endless free refills on the cold Coca-Colas at the grocery store café, or just sitting in the lobby of our bank, soaking up as much free air-conditioning as possible because we could no longer afford the electric bill on our big house. "And seeing how things are," I continued, "do you think you could see your way clear to sending me some money?"

"What was that, darling?" JoAnn asked. "You're speaking so softly I didn't quite catch your last question."

I knew from childhood experience that JoAnn's "darlings" could be devastating. One of the things that really drove me crazy about the women in Mother's family was their knack for making affection sound dangerous. They were, in general, people who rarely conveyed pure emotions: affection was cutting and anger was heartbreaking, and melancholy could be hilarious. ("Sad lives make funny people," JoAnn once told me.) The end result being that their finest moments were so tightly interwoven with their worst that when remembering happy times, it was nearly impossible not to remember miserable ones, too. "I asked if you could send me some money," I repeated.

"What, darling? I still didn't—"

"I said I need money. I'm desperate for money, and I need you to send me some."

"I see," said JoAnn. "But surely Bob's been required to provide some sort of financial support for you and your mother."

"Only fifteen hundred measly dollars a month. Which doesn't even begin to cover our expenses. And Daddy sends his check late every month, because he's trying to starve Mother into accepting a cheap divorce settlement."

"And you don't mean to suggest that the O'Dooles aren't offering you their assistance?" JoAnn asked. "It is, after all, their horse to which your mother has hitched her wagon."

Honestly, I didn't blame JoAnn a bit for savoring this phone call. From the moment Mother first started dating Daddy, she practically never saw her parents again. There'd been entire semesters when she hadn't come home from Texas A&M. Almost immediately, she'd begun spending holidays with Daddy's family, trying to worm her way into the O'Dooles' good graces. Once, she even moved without telling her parents—out of a dorm room they continued to pay for, and into an apartment with my father. "Hello, Shylock," JoAnn said to Mother, after finally tracking her down on the telephone. "Hello, Sherlock," Mother answered. I think JoAnn must have been sitting by the phone for years, waiting to be told Mother's life had come to grief.

But I suspected that if I wanted a check, this wasn't the ideal time to delve into our family history with JoAnn. So I stuck to the O'Dooles and answered: "They haven't given us so much as a dime. Nana and Papa haven't even sent Linda by with a casserole. I mean, can you contemplate that kind of cruelty? When they live right across the pasture. And all summer long, Mother and I've passed their cars on the road. And they act like we're not even living here. In your whole life, have you ever even *heard* of anybody being so mean to a member of their own family?"

JoAnn cleared her throat. "And in twenty years of marriage, your parents haven't saved any money at all? They don't own anything they can sell?"

"Only the house. Mother's lawyer told her that if she wants to get any money at all, she's going to have to let Nana and Papa buy her out of it. So that means we're going to have to find a new place to live. Which will probably be some crummy lead-painted cinder block apartment with core doors. And I just know that the second we move out, Daddy and Pam, and all their little illegitimate, bastard love children are moving in, because in a world like ours, the vulgar always seems to overtake the elegant. Don't you agree?"

JoAnn said she didn't have an opinion to offer on that point, but she did express a particular interest in Pam. "And what does your Mother have to say about this Pam woman?"

"She calls her *Trigger*."

"Because she looks like Roy Rogers's horse, or because your Mother wants to shoot her?"

"I'm not sure. But I know *I'd* like to shoot Pam. After all, she's really the one to blame for Mother acting so crazy and our being so poor."

"Robert, has it ever occurred to your mother that she might get a job?"

I couldn't speak for Mother, but before her plastic surgery, *I'd* begged Mother to get a job. "Don't be so shortsighted, Robert," Mother had replied. "A job would only interfere with my dating. And dating is, after all, where the real money's coming from." But this was not the answer I gave my grandmother. What I told JoAnn was that Mother was considering taking up social work.

"And what about you?" JoAnn asked.

"What about me?" I answered.

"Why don't you have a job? Or are you going to tell me you've also devoted your life to the poor and the needy?"

"Mother says getting straight A's is my job."

"The Mexican boy who does my yard was just elected president of his high school debate society, and he trims my crepe myrtles for two-fifty an hour."

"Well, I wasn't raised to do manual labor," I said. "And as for your lawn boy, I think it's much harder to have had something, and then to lose it, than never to have had it at all." Which was something I'd recently spent quite some time mulling over.

"Well, maybe that's true. But it seems to me that right now, you could use the two-fifty."

"Listen, JoAnn," I leveled. "I need your help. Can you send money, or can't you?"

"I'll see what I can spare."

"Thank you," I said. "Because right now, our life is what Mother would call a *pig fuck*. Meaning it's the absolute worst ever."

"I know what 'pig fuck' means, Robert. Your mother did not coin pig fuck. 'Pig fuck' belongs to *my* mother, and *your* great-grandmother Eugenia. But it figures Jessica would have appropriated it, because it sounds like she's turning into the spitting image of my mother—another mantrap who considered changes in lipstick color in terms of potential financial gain." Then JoAnn told me she had to get off the telephone. But before she did, I asked if maybe I could come visit her sometime, at her house in the Houston suburbs.

"You mean you'd like to come by and pick up your check? The mail works mighty fine, Robert. Bye now, darling," she said. And before I could say another word, she hung up.

I was exhausted. JoAnn's last "darling" had really stung. Even though I'd called her for the money, I had missed my grandmother—and going over to JoAnn and Alfred's house. Their life seemed exotic after Nana and Papa's ranch. Mother's parents lived in a small beach house they'd built on a golf course. Its walls were mostly glass, and the only drapes were in the bedrooms, so at night, the house twinkled with lights and movement. My grandparents' house was surrounded by fake Tudors and California-ranch-styles; and if I thought it sparkled glamorously at night, it was also true that it was, at all hours, transparent. Anyone in the neighborhood or the golf course could see whatever went on inside. "Why'd you ever build a beach house on a golf course?" Mother complained to JoAnn for years. "It's like living in a TV set."

"I guess I always wanted to live on the beach," my grandmother said.

On the days I'd spent as a small child at JoAnn's house,

she taught me show tunes on her player piano. I'd loved putting my arm around her waist while we sang together on the piano bench, and running my fingers over the smooth fabric of the A-line dresses she'd had cut from Courrèges patterns, in order to emphasize her very slight resemblance to Jackie Kennedy. I loved JoAnn's low, throaty laughter, like Tallulah Bankhead's: "HaHaHaHaHa." Which was how she often laughed after we finished a song and the roll on the player piano started spinning and flapping against the wood.

JoAnn was a terror in an A-line dress. Though she vaguely resembled Jackie Kennedy, the person she really looked like was Mother, in a brunette wig. Because Mother and JoAnn wore the same French perfume, they even smelled alike, although the scent seemed heavier and muskier on JoAnn. Mother and JoAnn, and Eugenia, too, for that matter, wore wigs and gold charm bracelets, and had voices that could rattle houses. They all dreamed of money, and each was absolutely furious that her fortunes seemed to ricochet back and forth between poverty and affluence, with the affluence never sticking quite so well as the poverty.

Before the Civil War, there had been twelve cotton plantations between Mother's families, the Peacocks and the Wilsons. Until World War II finally broke the cotton system, and nearly bankrupted my grandfather's family, the Wilsons continued to operate the plantation that covered most of the prized river-bottom land in the Brazos Valley near Bryan, Texas. But by the late 1950s, from their twelve plantations, Mother's family had managed to save lots of old rosewood furniture, crystal, monogrammed silver, and good, pretty etchings, but not one dollar. And it had taken every bit of my grandparents' money to build their house in the Houston suburbs.

Mother's great-aunt Hazel, who had perhaps murdered her rich husband with a poisoned pina colada, was the family's sole, lucky exception where money was concerned. Much more typical was her grandmother, Eugenia Peacock, who was, according to JoAnn, Mother's spitting image. Eugenia—who authored an antifeminist treatise entitled *I's Tired a Libbin'*, which argued that women have always run the world through puppet and purse strings—married and divorced at least six men, without collecting a farthing from any of them in alimony or property. I say that my great-grandmother was married to "at least" six men, because Eugenia never shared with anybody the exact number—sometimes yanking a new ex-husband out of her past, like an earring from the bottom of an old purse.

One of Eugenia's ex-husbands, Buck Buchanan, was the warden of Huntsville State Prison, and while she was married to him, Eugenia had the benefit of raiding the women's prison for domestic help. Though Buck always tried to score the coveted nonviolent offenders for his wife's lady's maids, Eugenia wouldn't hear of it. "Buck," she demanded, "don't bring me home some petty thief who'll rob me blind. A pickpocket is always a pickpocket. Bring me some poor black woman serving life for murdering her husband. She'll never repeat the crime, because you can't kill your husband twice. And besides, chances are the son of a bitch needed killing." It had been one of Eugenia's Housekeepers

Who'd Murdered Her Husband who'd taught JoAnn and Mother how to burn green candles and pray to Jesus for a man's "removal" to heaven.

Eugenia always moved into JoAnn's spare room when she was between husbands. But she never stayed long because she found JoAnn's life in the suburbs, forever married to my grandfather, Alfred Wilson, too dull. For her failure to divorce Alfred in order to pursue other, wealthier men, Eugenia numbered JoAnn a defeated woman. "Just because your first husband didn't strike it rich, JoAnn, doesn't mean you can't go right out and find one who did. You got to get back on that horse, honey pie. I mean, do you have any idea how it makes a mother's heart ache to see her daughter wallowing in defeat?"

JoAnn was, herself, a flamboyant personality. But something—whether it had been the loss of the Wilsons' plantation or Eugenia's checkered romantic past—had inspired in her a certain amount of caution in her relationships to money and men. She'd worked hard in her quiet, suburban marriage to my grandfather. By keeping their life small, my grandparents were able to live well. Alfred made a good salary designing oil pipelines. JoAnn drove a succession of Cadillacs, and had a housekeeper, and was the only woman in her family who always kept money in her savings account. And though JoAnn loved Alfred (theirs was really the only successful union in Mother's family), she was just as furious as the other Peacock women about the lack of wealth and glamour in her life. Except JoAnn's anger didn't rage like Eugenia's. It fizzled into depression, and if JoAnn was not, as her mother had accused her, defeated, then she was resigned—to a suburban life and marriage very different from that which she'd imagined.

For as long as Mother was resigned to her life on Nana and Papa's ranch, and to her marriage to my father, I'd believed that, out of all the women in her family, she most resembled JoAnn. But since she'd recently become reinvigorated, she reminded me more and more of the stories I'd heard about Eugenia. I had, in fact, hoped to appeal to my grandmother's checkbook on the basis of family tradition and the common impossibility of our mothers.

Mother, too, was not unaware that she was following in her grandmother's footsteps—an idea that terrified her. After a series of impulsive divorces, Eugenia had been forced to spend the final years of her life in JoAnn's guest room, broke and miserable, and finally unable to live according to the advice she'd bombarded Mother with as a small girl: "Marry money, Jessica. And if that doesn't work, then get a divorce. And then, marry money again."

Since Mother had been forced to witness Eugenia's pitiful end, she was afraid that she, too, would eventually end up living in *my* spare room, without the means to purchase an entire coordinated outfit off one of the mannequins in the store window at Neiman Marcus. This had become Mother's ultimate gauge of squalor. Since Daddy had left us in June, and particularly during that period when we'd lived off the return of Mother's coordinated outfits to department stores across Houston, Mother's fear of reliving her grandmother's fate had loomed large before her: "My grandmother told me, Robert, that the only time she'd ever been able to afford to march into a department store and buy an entire outfit—down to the pocketbook—right off the model was when she was married to a man. Oh, sure, as a single woman she had the wherewithal to purchase the odd blouse. A belt. A string of beads. But, never, never the whole, glorious, assembled-by-the-Neiman's-window-designer ensemble. Oh, Robert. Pray no such future awaits me."

And imagining Mother spending her last days in the spare room of my future home, I did pray—for myself, and Mother, and for the safe delivery of whatever rich man awaited her.

CHAPTER SEVEN

Crazy Glue

"I've got to get a move on with Mr. Taft," Mother said, sitting in bed, leaning into the lamp light, and trying to spot-clean a pancake makeup stain on the Peter Pan collar of her best white dress. It was a few days after my telephone conversation with JoAnn and just a week after the surgeries. Mother was frowning, at least as much as her lips would allow. They were still bruised blue—swollen and sticking straight out, like a duck's bill. "We can't even afford dry-cleaning. Mark my words, Robert. It's not long now before the squalor shows." Except, what she really said was that she didn't have long before the "thqualor showth," which made me, alternately, want to giggle and sob.

Mother had refused to allow her matrimonial future, newly brightened by silicone implants, to be postponed by her convalescence. She'd been out of bed as soon as she could bear it, chewing pain pills like licorice drops, hobbling around the house in her peignoir, and cupping her bulging breasts in her elbow while trying to walk in a way that wouldn't make her new chest jiggle. And though her newly broadened body wasn't fit for public exhibition, she'd already begun scheduling romantic dinners and theater dates with Mr. Taft, her most likely groom-to-be. In order to prepare Mr. Taft for the drastic changes in her appearance, Mother had lied to him, telling him that her gynecologist had prescribed new birth control pills that caused "just a dab of water retention" in her lips and breasts. "He's never going to believe that in a million years," I'd told her. But, Mother disagreed: "A man will believe anything, any lie at all, that has to do with a woman'th monthly vithitor."

During her brief period of bed rest, in those heady days immediately following her surgeries, Mother had done some heavy thinking—deciding that only baldness stood between her and blissful matrimony. Though she had, for years, supplanted her sickly, dandelion-fuzz hair with luxurious blond wigs, she'd recently formed the opinion that, in certain intimate positionings unavoidable on the long path to the altar, wearing a wig would prove awkward. So, after we saw a commercial on *Good Morning, Houston* for an experimental hair salon that claimed to perform miracles on women with thinning hair, and sold Crème de la Mer wholesale, I wasn't surprised when Mother idly asked me, on the final day of my summer vacation, if I'd mind taking a drive into town.

"We're going to that hair salon we saw on TV, aren't we?" I asked her.

"I'd drive mythelf, but I'm recovering from thurgery," Mother said.

"You're in no better shape to have your hair done than you are to drive. Why not just wait until you feel a little better? Then, we'll go back to Neiman's, and see what Eduardo might be able to do for you. He's done your hair for years."

"I'm beyond Eduardo'th help, Robert. I don't need a hairdrether. I need a miracle worker. Mr. Taft can never be allowed to know that I wear a wig."

"Why not?" I asked. "You wear a wig; he wears a toupée. You two seem like the perfect couple."

"It'th not the thame thing at all, and you know it. I want womanly hair—luthiouth, thintillating hair—and I need to hide the fact that I've thinned a little on top."

Long-term bleaching had caused Mother's scalp to look like one of those Russian potato fields that you see in the *National Geographic*, razed and scorched in order to regenerate the nutrients in the soil. "Well, Mother, you've done more than thin a little on top. You're bald. So, how, exactly, are these miracle workers going to provide you with this luscious, scintillating hair?"

Mother's face took on that steely-eyed Captain Ahab expression she so often made while discussing cosmetics and beauty treatments. "Never you mind every little detail," she said, tossing a ringless hand. "I've told you the truth, and now, your Mother needth your thupport!" Mother said this in a way that implied that she expected my gratitude for not telling me, this time, that she was hemorrhaging from one of her various orifices. There was no stopping Mother. I knew that if I didn't drive her, she'd most likely try to do it herself. Or, much worse, she'd call and ask Eddie, reviving a friendship in which Mother had seemed to be losing interest.

So, I helped Mother hoist her aching body into the Jaguar, stuffing sofa pillows under her chest and arms to absorb road bumps. Even still, Mother grimaced every time we hit a pothole. And when I had to slam on the brakes to avoid hitting a Datsun pickup with a flat rear tire, she looked like she was in the throes of agony.

It took nearly two hours of anguished driving to find Mother's new hair salon. It was located next door to a pet hotel in a strip mall with a tarred parking lot, right off the Southwest Freeway. There was a Gulf station at the end of the complex nearest the freeway exit, and a billboard sign, advertising the salon, towered over its rooftop, picturing a barefoot woman on a rope swing, curling her toes in the sunlight. The woman shook a thick mane of chestnut hair through the spring breeze, as though she were drying it like laundry: hers was a prime example of the luscious, scintillating hair Mother so desired.

Mother had stashed a wad of pain pills in the front pocket of her big cotton blouse, and by the time we hit the Interstate she was openly chewing them, one after the other. Even the way Mother chewed her pills looked painful. Between chews, she'd press her mouth with one of the homemade ice packs they'd shown her how to make at the plastic surgeon's: latex gloves filled with cold water and shaved ice, and packed until they looked like cow udders.

Perhaps it was the pain pills, but the effect of the billboard on Mother was mesmerizing. Pulling herself from the car, she leaned back against the passenger's-side door, and stared up at it in pure wonder and longing. "Look, Robert," she said. "Will you thimply look at all that hair?! Ithn't it marvelouth? Now I athk you, ith there anything on earth more thimply gorgeouth than hair like that?" Mother's voice was tender and whispery, as though she'd seen a vision, as though she believed her maker had led her to the single patch of earth upon which she was meant to stand.

It was almost noon, and the August sun was so strong it bleached the midday white. The back of the silk shirt I wore was soaked through, heavy with sweat, and the parking lot seemed to be melting away beneath our feet. While Mother stared in rapture at the billboard advertisement, the dangerous smells of the freeway—gasoline and tar and melting rubber—made it all but impossible to discern the chemical aroma of dye and permanent-wave solution wafting from the hair salon. The blare of police sirens and the whoosh of cars made it difficult to hear the yelp and howl of the dogs imprisoned in the pet hotel next door.

From the heat, and from the fire of her mission, Mother, too, seemed to be melting. (And considering the very large proportion of her body now consisting of petroleum products, this fate seemed likely indeed.) "These people must have scraped together every last nickel to buy that commercial on *Good Morning, Houston,*" I said. Mother finally managed to take her eyes away from the sign, slamming the car door shut, and hitching her purse onto her shoulder. Both actions looked painful: she reached into the pocket of her blouse, and began chewing another pill. "And I don't think the best time to have one's hairstyle radically altered is while overdosing on prescription medication. Especially not in a shithole like this. I think we should call Neiman's, get Eduardo on the phone, and see if he can recommend some better place."

"Jethuth Chritht, Robert! Let up on me, will you? Don't be frightened by the neighborhood. I've checked everything out over the telephone. The people who work here approach a woman'th hair like an art form. They innovate. They exthperiment. The lady on the phone exthplained that they've worked very hard to avoid public attention. They fly under the radar, tho they can cater to a very thelect clientele. Do you know that they told me that they do the hair of—" Here Mother leaned in and whispered the name of a famous Houston socialite who'd recently been awarded an enormous divorce settlement from her oil baron husband. "Okay? Doethn't that reathure you? Your old Mother'th got everything under control. Now, thtop critithizing me!"

"If they want to avoid publicity, then why do they advertise on TV?" I asked. Mother didn't answer. She just clutched her cow udder ice pack to her mouth like a lace handkerchief and headed towards the salon. I followed her through the door, thinking how very unlikely it seemed that that socialite, whose hair always looked quite lovely in the Style section of the *Houston Chronicle*, had ever visited this strip mall. The entry to the salon was dim and cool, and I was blind while my eyes adjusted to the light. The first thing I saw, upon regaining my vision, was distasteful. A large woman named Shirley, who had the figure of a mashed potato, sat behind a wicker table watching

McMillan and Wife on a rabbit-ear television and eating ice out of a Taco Bell cup with her bare fingers.

As we approached her desk, Shirley looked annoyed that we were disturbing her program. "No, sir," she sighed, as she lowered the set's volume, keeping her fingers, still wet from the ice-cubes, poised on the knob, ready to turn it back up as soon as she was rid of us. "There'll never be another Rock Hudson." She glanced at Mother. "You the twelve o'clock treatment?"

"Yeth," said Mother. "I believe I am." The situation seemed undeserving of the enthusiasm in Mother's voice.

"Well, hon, like I told you on the phone, we take our money up front. And we deal in cash dollars." Mother was prepared for this; she reached into her purse and handed Shirley a fat envelope of twenty-dollar bills, which Shirley began counting aloud, interrupting herself to reach into her paper cup and toss a few more squares of ice into the side of her mouth. "They just made me quit smokin' at my desk," she explained, "on account of all the fake hair in this place being so flammable. Said I might catch the whole waxworks on fire. That's how come I'm eatin' all this ice. For the oral stimulation. Heard about it on the talk radio."

"We underthtand completely," said Mother. She said this very quickly, I noticed, as though she wished to prevent me from commenting on Shirley's withdrawal process. Mother needn't have feared. I was too distracted by my surroundings to speak. The lobby was decorated with patio furniture. Shirley's desk, the chairs, the coffee table, everything was wicker. Rather than art, the walls were covered with posters, thumb-tacked into the drywall. *Well, we've come a long way from Neiman Marcus* was all I could say to myself.

"Okay, it's all there," Shirley said. She'd counted out over a thousand dollars in twenties—bills that represented the final few carats of Mother's diamond rings. Then Shirley shuffled the money back into its envelope and stuffed it into her jeans pocket.

"Oh," said Mother, "you can't let me forget. I hope there ithn't a limit to how much of that wholethale Crème de la Mer you'll thell me. Becauthe I want to buy a lot of it."

"Crème de who?" asked Shirley.

The moan of some sorrowful dog crept through the wall from the pet hotel. "Never mind," said Mother. Then, Shirley handed Mother a receipt that was wrinkled and drippy from Shirley's fat, wet fingers. She looked at Mother's lips and, while squinting her eyes, looked at me, and then back at Mother's lips—as if she couldn't quite make up her mind whether Mother had just had plastic surgery or I'd beaten her.

Finally, Shirley threw back another fistful of ice before standing up and leading us down a hall with a fluorescent light that buzzed and flickered, and into a little room in the back about the size of a kitchen appliance. The room had been filled by an ancient barber's chair, with stainless-steel head and leg rests. It was so large they must have built the walls around it. "Your beauty technician'll be right with you," said Shirley. She waved Mother towards the chair and rushed back to her desk to catch the opening credits of *Hart to Hart*, the theme music of which she pronounced to be her favorite song.

"Mother, I can't imagine anyone from the Style section setting foot in this place. Not even Georgette Mosbacher. What sort of 'miracles' do they claim to work here anyway? Weaves, extensions, something like that?"

"Umm-hmm," said Mother. "Thomething like that." The pain medication had begun to settle over Mother like a cloud, and even when she spoke directly to me, her eyes seemed to shift in and out of focus as if she couldn't quite make out my face.

Just then, Mother's new stylist walked into the room, a woman who called herself Veronique, which seemed very unlikely. I tried to imagine what Eduardo would think of her, and I could only imagine he'd cross the street to avoid acknowledging someone so lowly who deigned to number herself a member of his profession. After all, Veronique wore pedal pushers, a Mickey Mouse T-shirt, and pink foam flip-flops. Which would have, under normal circumstances, when Mother was saner and sober, caused her to grab her handbag, and my elbow, and demand her money back. Mother considered the wearing of flip-flops anyplace other than the beach to be a symbol of Western decay so profound that social disintegration on the level of the final days of Rome couldn't be far behind. "Quality people," Mother had always said, "do not wear Styrofoam shoes." But despite the chipped polish on Veronique's toes, and the dry skin cracking on her heels, Mother smiled expectantly, as though something wonderful was about be delivered to her. This was probably because Veronique, to give credit where it's due, had one of the most glorious heads of hair I'd ever seen: She utterly shamed the brunette on the rope swing in the salon's billboard advertisement. Limp, heavy-hanging ringlets of copper-colored hair bounced from Veronique's head with a slow liquid grace every time she moved her clumsy, naked feet. It was highlighted in a sparkling, prismatic way, like sunbeams dancing in a swimming pool. It was both luscious *and* scintillating, and despite her Mickey Mouse T-shirt, it made Veronique a ringer for the Botticelli Venus.

With Veronique in the room, the space became too crowded. I leaned into the doorframe and glanced over at Mother's swirly eyes, which were dulled and bedazzled from the combined effects of pain pills and Veronique's hair. I realized her mind was far, far away from any objection so mundane as Styrofoam footwear. "Oh," Mother gasped, "I love your hair. Did you have it done here?"

"Nope, darlin'. God's gift to me. Ev'body who walks through that door asks me that question, though."

For a brief moment, Mother looked like she was going to cry. But the dream carried her forward. As soon as Veronique began removing the pins that held Mother's wig, she seemed fully recovered and expectant of miracles.

Having lifted it from her head, Veronique cast Mother's wig down on the Rubbermaid wheelie tray that held her supplies, in the manner of a religious healer throwing down the crutches of a redeemed cripple. "You won't be needin' *this* no more. Not after today anyway, darlin'." The wall in front of the barber's chair was covered with mirrors, and in it, I watched Veronique's eyes dart, quite suspiciously, between Mother's lips and me. She must have decided that I didn't look like a bruiser and that Mother was recovering from plastic surgery, because as she started her work, a slow groping of Mother's naked scalp, Veronique began speaking to Mother in a low, cooing voice. "Well, aren't you a pretty little thing. A pretty, pretty little thing." And joining eyes with me in the mirror, she asked, "Isn't your mama a pretty little thing?"

Now, in general, yes, I think my mother is a beautiful woman. But, at that particular moment, with her head, which had grown a bit limp from the pills, being supported in Veronique's hands in that dingy back room, with the few, staticky strands of her hair slowly waving up from her scalp, her eyes milky and dull, and her mangled blue lips seeming bluer still under the buzzing fluorescent lights, Mother looked like the Curse of the Cat People. But I managed to gulp, say a quick prayer to Jesus, and nod. "Yes, Veronique, my mother *is* a pretty little thing."

Then, moving her fingers over Mother's scalp, Veronique began taking a series of rapid measurements, with the abstract look of a seamstress sizing up a bosom. Releasing Mother's head and leaning back, she cocked her eye, sucked her thumbnail, and squinted at Mother. She said, under her breath, as though careful not to break her own concentration, "Now, I know that Shirley explained to you over the telephone how all this is going to work, right?"

Without Veronique's hands supporting it, Mother's head dipped a little to one side, and the pink tip of her tongue slipped a bit from the corner of her mouth. But as soon as Veronique spoke, she rallied. "Oh yeth," Mother said. "I completely underthtand."

"And you're not having second thoughts or nothin.'

'Cause, you know, what we're doing can't be undone for a while."

"Looking forward to it," said Mother, giving another glimpse towards the glinting, fire-dappled, penny-colored fountain that was Veronique's hair.

I kept hoping Veronique would have to step out of the room for a moment, so I could grill Mother on what, exactly, she was having done to her hair. But Veronique was lost in her work, brushing the sad remains of Mother's stiff, scraggy, blond hair straight back, so that it stood suspended, as though held there by the wind. Then, she began to trim Mother's hair, short.

For a while, I lost interest. As my legs began to tire and ache, standing in the doorframe, my mind wandered. I traced, with my eyes, the tattoo on Veronique's ankle: a treble clef drawn in bright purple ink, and filled in with blue. I began wishing for a chair, and arching my back, and yawning, and stretching my arms above my head. I began to think of walking to the Gulf station to buy a Coca-Cola, and wondered if a novel or an old *Vogue* might be stashed in the floorboards of Mother's Jag. The cool, damp air-conditioning of the salon began to lull me. I felt heavy and limp, and had almost settled on napping with Shirley in the salon's quiet lobby. But when Veronique removed a pair of electric shears from a Rubbermaid storage drawer, I found my interest piquing. Plugging her shears into a power strip, Veronique flipped the switch on and off a couple of times, and their metal teeth leapt to life with an electric, hungry purr.

Then, with a twinkle in her eye, Veronique turned

toward my mother's drooping head. I stepped forward and laid my hand on her arm. "Hey. What's with the clippers, Veronique?" I asked, trying hard to sound jokey and light-hearted.

"Oh," said Veronique, startled from the depth of her thoughts. She still held the shears closely over Mother's head, and their teeth seemed to lunge after the farthest strands of her hair. "I'm sorry. I thought we were all on the same page here. I'm going to shave off all your mother's hair." She said this in the same tone of voice as she might have said, "I'm going to breathe air." Then she switched her clippers off.

Mother's sad little head perked up. "Don't interfere, Robert." She waved me off with her cow udder ice pack, then reached into her purse, and grabbed at what must have been among her last dollars in the world. Tossing them at me, she said, "Go buy a magathine! Or go to a movie, or thomething. Jutht leave me alone!"

Ignoring Mother, I spoke directly to Veronique. "You're going to shave off all of my mother's hair?"

"Yeah, huh," said Veronique.

"For what purpose?"

"Veronique knowth what she'th doing, Robert," Mother said. "The woman ith a profethional." Again, I glanced down at Veronique's bare feet. Mother tried to push herself out of her chair, presumably to shoo me out of the room, but was too weak, and so began chewing another pain pill and pressing her ice pack to her forehead.

"I'm going to shave off all your pretty mama's hair, so's

I can glue a brand-spankin'-new head of hair right back on her." Again, she said this as she would say, "I'm going to eat food and drink water." Veronique still held her finger over the shears' power switch. It looked itchy to begin its work.

I nodded, then turned back to Mother, trying to wedge myself between her and Veronique. "Mother," I said. I spoke slowly. "You understand you are here to have all of your hair shaved off, so that Veronique here [I cast my eyes up to heaven] can super-glue new, fake hair onto your bald scalp."

"Don't talk to me like I'm thtupid or thomething," said Mother. "I know why I'm here." Mother tried to push me away and began apologizing to Veronique for me.

Veronique patted me on the shoulder with the hand that wasn't holding the electric clippers, and began guiding me out of the room. "Now, we're gonna make your mama look real nice, so don't you worry 'bout a thing."

As I shook off Veronique's hand, I saw Mother begin chewing another pill, and this time, taking a swig out of an Evian bottle from her purse that was, probably, at least ninety proof. "So from now on," I said, "my mother's going to have to shave her head every morning, before crazy-gluing fake hair back on?"

"Course not. We use *super* strong glue. It's long-lasting, and guaranteed to stay stuck for at least a couple of weeks. 'Til your mother comes back for her next appointment. Then, we'll peel her new hair off, reshave her scalp, let it breathe for a little while, and reapply. In the meantime, she can shower and swim . . . and"—and this Veronique said very slowly—"she could even ride back and forth 'cross Houston in a convertible if she wanted to."

Mother nodded her head enthusiastically.

"Mother . . . ," I said. I tried to meet Mother's eyes, but couldn't. Then, I reached out to touch Mother's hand, but as I did, Veronique drew a fresh blond wig of artificial hair, a couple of shades yellower than Mother's usual color, from the top drawer of the Rubbermaid wheelie. She shook the wig, and a ripple of fluorescent light ran through it. Mother's eyes darted with the light, charmed like a crow before a piece of tinfoil. Following Mother's eyes, I knew she was as good as sheared.

"Fine," I said. "But I'm not going anywhere. I'm staying right where I am, and watching the whole damn thing."

Veronique grinned a bit, and the clippers charged back to life in her hand. Then, in careful rows, she shaved my mother bald. Mother's scalp was startlingly white, and, without hair, she looked so pitiful, like a blue-lipped baby bird. Veronique seemed eager to distract her from looking at herself in the mirror. So she started asking Mother questions like: how long had she been bald, and what life experiences had she been denied for having been bald, and what had finally made her take this important, life-changing step, and what did she want her new hair to look like once they were finished, and how did she want her hair cut and styled? Mother shut her eyes and began a rambling, drunken monologue about Carole Lombard and Virna Lisi and Tippi Hedren and Cybill Shepherd—speaking in such a way that I could barely keep from crying from the longing in her voice.

As Mother talked, Veronique took a tiny squeezy bottle of something that looked remarkably like the crazy glue Daddy kept in his toolbox, but which she assured both of us wasn't poison, and began applying long, clear rows of it to Mother's scalp. And then, once again, Veronique picked up the blond wig that was to become Mother's new hair, even though it was yellow, and careful not to let its strands fall into the glue, she stuck its rubber scalp onto Mother's skull, and pressed down hard on Mother's head, as though she were trying to flatten it. "Honey," she said, "I got to make sure I get all the little air bubbles out from under this rubber. I learned that the hard way, how one little air bubble can spread until it makes its way across your whole head, and this hair just comes flying off. Now, we can't have that happenin' now, can we?" Mother's neck seemed on the verge of collapsing from all of Veronique's pushing. Perhaps it was the effect of the yellow hair on Mother's pale complexion, but her face looked a little green.

Finally, Veronique, with a gesture of triumph, said, "There now! Course we got to trim the ends a bit. But, in general, what do you think of the new you?"

Now, it was true that many of Mother's usual wigs didn't pass for real hair: They were fabulous, dramatic, extensions of her over-the-top personality and seemed absolutely right for her for that reason. But the hair Veronique glued onto Mother's head looked completely unrelated to her. It looked like it had been decoupaged to her scalp. It looked like she was wearing a yellow hat. It looked like a yellow muppet was sitting on her head.

Mother lifted Veronique's hand mirror and, tossing her head, began an attempt to discover her look's new, candid, fascinating angles. All the while, I kept thinking that it was remarkable how much greener the yellow hair made her skin look. Artfully, Mother mussed her hair, to lend it a windblown, devil-may-care appeal. Each time she tossed her hair, it produced a rustly, plastic sound, much like the shaking of a cheerleading pom-pom. Mother tried not to notice this, and continued to smile into the mirror in a way that looked like she was rapt in conversation and laughter. Then, Mother set Veronique's mirror in her lap and looked at herself in the long mirror on the wall. Her face cracked, and she opened her mouth, and I thought she would burst into tears. But instead, she vomited.

Mother threw up all over her lap, and all over her cow udder ice pack, and all over Veronique's hand mirror. Then, she turned to her left, and threw up all over Veronique's Rubbermaid wheelie. Then she attempted to stand, but was in too much pain to get up and vomit at the same time— so, she hunched into the big, metal chair and, leaning her head over the armrest, continued to throw up on the floor. Veronique tried, several times, to place a wastebasket under Mother's head, but each time she did, Mother attempted to thank her and narrowly missed vomiting all over her, too. Finally, Veronique set the wastebasket on the floor, and began to swivel Mother's chair, in order to position her head over the basket. But the chair wouldn't swivel that far, and all that swiveling just made Mother vomit even more. It also had the unfortunate effect of spreading the vomit all over the little room. Mother started yelling,

"Thtop thwiveling me!" Which made Shirley, the receptionist in need of oral stimulation, come running down the hall. Unwilling to enter the room, she stood beside me in the doorway, where I had remained, with my elbows tucked against my sides and my hands cupped over my mouth, too stunned to move. Shirley watched Mother throw up some more, and held her nose, and made *Puuuu-eeeey!* sounds, like she was calling the pigs home, and kept saying, "I sure am grateful I don't have to do the mopping around here. Boy oh boy, I sure am grateful for that."

And much later, long after the sheer mass of Mother's vomit had begun to seem supernatural, as though it were being produced magically by some source outside her body, Mother's stomach exhausted itself, and I began apologizing to Veronique. I explained to her that Mother was recovering from surgery and had taken too many pain pills. That she really shouldn't have had her hair done today, but that she had wanted to come so badly and was so looking forward to having new hair. I made a point of telling Veronique that Mother considered her to be both an artist and a miracle worker. Under the circumstances, Veronique, who I couldn't help but notice had vomit all over her bare feet, was noble. She filled an Astroworld coffee mug with cold water and gave it to Mother, stroking her back. "I've got twin boys in day care," she said to me, "and there's barely a day that goes by when one of them's not upchucking something or other."

"Well, that's lovely of you to say," I told her. Mother was still bent over the armrest, breathing very hard and moaning. Slowly, she pulled herself up, and began rummaging around in her purse for a package of moist towelettes. Her face had returned to its normal coloring, except, of course, for the blue lips, which, as she took another look at herself in the mirror, began to quiver. "Oh, I'm tho thorry, Veronique. I'm jutht tho, tho thorry," Mother said, taking slow sips from Veronique's coffee mug, while water dribbled down her chin. Then, she looked at herself in the mirror and started to cry at the sight of her new yellow hair, which had little dabs of vomit in it. "I wanted to be Carole Lombard, Veronique. I wanted glamorouth hair. All I ever wanted wath luthious, thintillating, glamorouth hair." Mother wiped her face with a moist towelette, and then began the task of scrubbing the vomit out of her hair with another, producing a squeaky, plastic sound, similar to wet sneakers on linoleum.

"I know, darlin', I know," said Veronique. "Everything's going to be alright. Everything's going to be alright, and you can come back anytime you like, and get your hair cut, and we'll make you look like a pretty little thing."

Veronique never stopped stroking Mother's back. Not when she led her, gently, through the puddles of her vomit, past Shirley and me, who were still standing in the door-way, and not when she took her into the bathroom, to wash up, and to, perhaps, find something else for her to wear on the long drive home. "I'm forty-five yearth old, and my huthband left me for a lady jockey, and now she'th pregnant, and all I ever wanted wath luthiouth hair, only now it'th yellow, and it thoundth like a pom-pom, and I've got to marry a man I find revolting and he liveth in Lubbock and hith idea of the theater ith Michael Flatley, Lord of the Danthe!" Mother wept all the way down the hall, and into the bathroom, and the only thing Veronique said was, "I know, darlin'. Everything is going to be alright."

Shirley slurped some of the water that still dripped down the side of her palm from the last ice cube she'd eaten, and let out a low whistle. "Couldn't pay me enough money. No sir, not enough money in the world to clear out that mess." She shook her head back and forth and slowly walked back down the hall. As I stood watching her slow, vegetable-like body move away from me, I listened to the dogs from the pet hotel howling through the walls, and I started to laugh until I shook, and wondered why Everything's Going to be Alright is always the perfect thing to say to a crying person, regardless of how improbable any sort of happy resolution to their problems may be. And I thought, as I borrowed a Hefty bag from Shirley, and began wrapping the passenger seat of Mother's Jaguar with it, in order to prevent her vomit from staining the leather, that there are no poor eccentrics. Money lends you a dignity that has nothing to do with who you are, but everything to do with the way you're treated, and that is, for what it's worth, extremely effective in silencing potato people like Shirley.

Veronique huddled Mother out of the salon, wrapped in one of those smocks you wear while you get your hair dyed. In the sunlight, Mother's hair shone like yellow Astroturf. She was still saying "I'm tho, tho thorry" to Veronique, who told me, "Keep your windows cracked, darlin', so's the odor don't get too strong for you on the Interstate. I got a brother-in-law lives out near where you live, and it's a long, long drive. And once your mama starts feelin' better, you remind her that I still owe her a hair trim."

"That's very considerate of you, Veronique," I said. "I suppose that if someone had to shave my mother's head, and then crazy-glue new, yellow plastic hair onto her bald scalp, and then watch her puke her brains out all over a room the size of a microwave oven because she's overdosed on pain medication, then I'm glad that that person was someone as sensitive and considerate as you are."

Veronique gave the low roof of Mother's car a couple of slaps, by way of saying good-bye, and walked back into the salon. Mother slumped, moaning, in the seat beside me. For a moment, I just sat there, without igniting the engine. Then I turned the car key and angled my nose into the clean air of the air conditioner, but kept the car in park, and tried, for a moment, to keep absolutely still, thinking of the old wisdom that says things are never as bad as they can get. Which, at the moment, seemed like gospel truth— tomorrow being, after all, the first day of school.

CHAPTER EIGHT

A Fool's Paradise

But actually, it was a relief to get back to Trinity Lutheran—my ambling and country-mannered Evangelical high school, where most of our time was spent, in theological terms, considering the lilies of the field. Trinity even had its own version of the siesta: an hourlong break period, which was supposed to be spent in prayer, but which I mostly spent napping in the long, unmowed grass of the courtyard. Daddy had been ordered by the judge to continue paying my tuition. So, for eight hours a day, I was given a rest from life with Mother—which, since her bruising had subsided, and sun exposure had dulled the yellow tone off her new plastic hair, had become a mad round of social engagements with Mr. Taft.

Besides sloth, I enjoyed attending Trinity Lutheran for two reasons. First, I, like Mother, was endowed with a religious worldview. Though our religious spirit differed, no doubt, in many important respects, from that of my teachers—those hokey, doughy zealots with dishwater hair and gray, sun-starved complexions the color of a dead tooth—we shared, between us, an abiding faith in Jesus. Mother had taught me that Jesus Hates a Vacuum. To us, the Lord was a grownup's Santa Claus, who'd bring us anything we liked, if only we asked for it and were good enough. And Mother and I knew we were *more* than good enough.

Which brings me to the other reason I loved Trinity: arrogance. Attending Trinity Lutheran, rather than the Petunia public school, made my sense of superiority so much easier to maintain. Trinity's students were, as Mother said, "a nicer class of people"—they lacked the meanness of poverty and weren't violent.

I'd sort of been driven out of public school after Junior High for being so fey, and also so flush with cash. I'd always had more money than my cowpoke classmates, and with it, I bought pastel pants. I had my hair streaked and my nails coated with a clear varnish as delicate as the lacquer on Chinese porcelain. Finding the school's air-conditioning weak, I carried, in my monogrammed suede book bag, aerosol spray cans of French water, sold in six-packs at Neiman's. The moment I felt a mere bead of sweat forming on my brow in, say, Texas History class, I'd reach down and mist myself. (And still, I didn't know I was gay—special, in some way involving flair and class and heat sensitivity, but not gay. Oy.) Need I say that, at Beckendorf Junior High, I was the object of mass violence?

My time in the Petunia public school system taught me the lesson every gay boy learns fast: that language is the weapon of the powerless; that if you reduce someone to tears in public, they probably won't beat you. It's a sink-or-swim mechanism I'd have likely inherited from Mother and JoAnn anyway, but I doubt it would have developed quite so early if my voice hadn't been pitched quite so high.

"You've got to kick 'em in the cunt," was Mother's advice when I came home crying because Barbie, the eighth-grade slut, or the Girl with the Gimpy Eye, said I talked like a fag. Mother said it was a Dominance of the Herd technique she'd picked up back when she was head cheerleader. During the day, while I was at school, Mother would spend long hours in bed, working up viperous retorts for me to use against anyone who threatened to have me pummeled by the football team. (The fact that boys almost never bullied me, while girls often threatened to *have* their boyfriends beat me, only contributed to my growing sense that men were ciphers, while women were quite fascinating people.) Sometimes, having devised some particularly devastating bit of dialogue, Mother would have me paged out of class to the office telephone. "I've got it," she'd say. "If that Barbie says anything to you today, you just say this. Say: *Barbie, your vagina is looser than the top on an old mayonnaise jar.* Don't you just love that? I worked all morning trying to get that right. And if you don't like that one, try: *When you open your mouth like that, Barbie darling, I can almost see your vulva.* Do you need to write that down, Robert? Isn't that wicked? She'll drop dead!"

Eventually, however, after I caused a girl whose acne made her face look like a topographical map of the state of

Arizona to dry-heave so hard she had to be sent to the nurse's station, Mother insisted I be transferred to Trinity out of fear for my life: "You can only mouth off like that so many times before they put your head on a stick," she said.

At Trinity Lutheran, my risk of suffering a hematoma was considerably lessened by the fact that my classmates were the unworldly and literal-minded children of religious fanatics, possessing a consciousness circa 1952. They thought gay people comprised some foreign species: I think it would have taken a tiara and cha-cha heels in order for them to have spotted me. And even if they had, I still wouldn't have needed Mother to script vicious one-liners, because Trinity kids were purely sweet, in that way people always are when they're afraid they'll rot in hell if they look sideways at you.

By the fall of 1996, Mother was busy writing her own material, for a new act without an obvious role for me to play. I turned seventeen in mid-September, an age when everyone feels suddenly confronted by adulthood. But as Mother's new life began taking her away from me—on weekend trips with Mr. Taft that gradually, as the autumn passed, grew longer, spreading through the weeks—a unique pressure began to be exerted upon me, having nothing to do with my age, to embrace the freedom of adulthood.

Mr. Taft wanted me to hit the road. He wanted to marry Mother and move her to Lubbock, and I was the only thing holding up his proposal. I was too dense to understand immediately that I'd become a romantic liability for Mother;

that a middle-aged *jeune fille* can't be flanked by her grown son; that a rich man doesn't marry a blonde in order to support her children. And one of the reasons I failed to interpret the signals telling me that my days of living with Mother were numbered—signals such as the fact that during lulls in conversation Mr. Taft fell into the following refrain, "So your mama says it won't be long now before you move far, far away to a four-year college all the way up in New York City!"—was that I worked hard to avoid Mr. Taft's company. So hard, in fact, that I failed to notice he was also avoiding mine.

There were many good reasons for wanting to avoid Mr. Taft, and most of them were simply matters of good taste. The man wore wrinkle-resistant pants. His favorite weekend pastime was reenacting Civil War battles. He carried pictures of his tomato plants around in his wallet like they were his grandchildren. And every time he pulled his Cadillac out of a parking space, every time, he said the same thing: "We're off to see the Wizard!" Which was tolerable enough the first dozen or so times, but which eventually brought tears to my eyes.

But the real reason I avoided Mr. Taft had nothing to do with any of this, or the fact that he referred to Lubbock as "the old country," or even that he forced people to listen to Irish step dancing on his car stereo—something that was, to my mind, of dubious visual entertainment, but which held absolutely no aural appeal. No, the real reason I loathed spending time with Mr. Taft was the M&M (Moonlight and Magnolia) Act Mother put on whenever she was with him.

Mother's M&M Act was the same old Chase Him 'Til He's Caught You method of man-trapping usually employed by southern ladies. It consisted of Mother batting her false eyelashes and claiming, loudly and often, how passionately she loved listening to Irish step dancing on the radio, and asking, "Is anybody else hot in here?" when what she meant was, "Turn on the fucking air conditioner!" until Mr. Taft was finally convinced that Mother's every thought, opinion, and hobby were identical to his own. In a nutshell, the M&M Act involved Mother feeding Mr. Taft one completely unbelievable lie after the next, all of which he swallowed like gravy, because, I realized, gentlemen in the South expect ladies to lie to them out of feminine delicacy. But Mother wasn't lying because she was a lady. Mother was lying because she wanted all of Mr. Taft's money, and then, she wanted him to die.

"Remember," Mother warned me, one Saturday that fall, heading to my birthday luncheon at the Ritz—which really wasn't my birthday luncheon at all, but just a date I'd been invited to join at the last minute because Mother had guilt pangs for having been stuck, on my real birthday, in an airport with Mr. Taft while returning from a wine-tasting tour of the Sonoma Valley—"Mr. Taft thinks I'm fortyish."

"How *ish*?" I asked.

"Oh, you know," she said. "He thinks I'll be forty in, you know. . . ." Mother waved her hand in the air, as if to suggest the far horizon. "The next several years."

"Just how *ish* does that make me?" I asked.

"Don't mention your age."

"But what if he asks me? It *is* my birthday luncheon, sort of. Don't you think he's going to ask me how old I am?"

"Then just change the subject, Robert. Start talking about something else. But don't mention the O'Dooles. Or the divorce. Or the French. Or JoAnn and Alfred. And, whatever you do, for chrissakes, don't mention Jimmy Carter."

"Then what am I supposed to talk about?"

"Why don't you just stick to how much you want to move to New York? That's *always* safe. Just talk about moving away."

But mostly I tried not to talk, even when Mr. Taft asked me dumb, direct questions like whether Houston was hot enough for me, because I was so uncertain as to which basic facts of our life Mr. Taft was aware of, and so afraid of accidentally exposing Mother in a lie, that I just nodded my head and smiled at him like a foreign person, first over my mesclun salad and then over my fresh Gulf catfish, and finally over my *tres leches* cake.

It was Mother who kept the chatter breezing across the table—saying things like how lucky we were to have Mr. Taft escorting us to lovely restaurants, and how Mr. Taft always knew how to treat a lady, and how Mr. Taft had sworn to take her all the way to Virginia for a restaging of The Second Battle of Manassas. "Isn't that just too, too thrilling, Robert? Especially since you know that's always been my *very* favorite battle. So much better than The First Manassas, I've always thought."

Mr. Taft tugged proudly at the waist of his sans-a-belt pants. Between the wine and the cake and Mother's bragging, he looked baked and turkey-stuffed. And after he signed for his American Express card, Mother reached both of her hands across the table to hold both of Mr. Taft's hands, and mouthed "I love you" over the coffee service. And as he mouthed "I love you" back, his eyes positively sparkled with adoration and chardonnay, and Mother's charm bracelets tinkled in a way which, I'm sure, to Mr. Taft, sounded dainty and enticing, but which reminded me of the jangling of bullet casings. So that by the time we made it back to Mother's car, I was so exhausted by the effort of their romance that I napped all the way home.

Mother, too, was worn by her romance. She'd started smoking again (a habit she'd abandoned while modeling at Texas A&M) in order to cope with the fact that Mr. Taft's idea of perfect happiness was spending every spare minute alone with her. Even if Mother hadn't found him so repulsive—"Mr. Taft has strange tastes, Robert," was all she'd say—Mother's husbandly ideal had always run along the lines of incarcerated white-collar criminals and other high-dollar men prevented by circumstance from hanging around too much. Many times, over the years, I'd caught her gazing cow-eyed over a mug shot in the *Houston Chronicle* of some top oil executive ensnared by an insider-trading sting operation.

"Here's the plan, Robert," Mother said. "I'm marrying this old man. And then, I'm going to go to bed and smoke for the next fifty years." Mother said this to me while sitting in bed and smoking one cigarette, and then another, mashing their butts into the cut-crystal ashtray she'd propped onto her lap, which was the size of a hubcap and heavy enough to kill a man. This was how she spent most of her time between travels with Mr. Taft. And although I was disturbed by Mother's new passion for doing nothing (because it suggested a depressed state of mind, and because Mother's hair was so flammable, and because I'd been raised on the tale of The Fiery Death of Linda Darnell, who'd been Mother's favorite brunette movie star), I loved having the opportunity to sit on her bed and talk at her, as she leaned into her pillows, smoking with her eyes closed. I was still friendless, and Mother was still the only person listening to me. The less I saw of her, the more I had to tell her: about the movies, and about My New Idol, Lillian Hellman, and about Mrs. Rayburn, my geometry teacher, who I thought might be evil, but who did community theater musicals, which I thought might be fun.

One day in October, when my voice and Mother's cigarette smoke filled her bedroom, and I was attempting to convey just how fervently I wished Jesus would send me a famous, blacklisted writer to fall in love with, as he'd done for Lillian Hellman, Mr. Taft telephoned Mother, once more, to say how he couldn't wait for their weekend in Oaxaca. Then Mother began a truly disgusting routine of purring into the telephone receiver, and tut-tut-tutting her tongue, and just when I thought she'd hum a few bars from "My Heart Belongs to Daddy," she made a series of noises with her lips that sounded like she was calling the mallards home to roost, and then she hung up. "God," she said. "Even the telephone is hateful."

"All I have to say is Mr. Taft is no Dashiell Hammett," I said, because I wanted to make sure our earlier conversation wasn't sidetracked.

"Well, Mr. Taft is the best hope we've got right now," said Mother. She squished a cigarette into her ashtray like she was trying to kill a bug. "Although, when I asked the Lord for a husband, *he* was not what I had in mind."

"Which is why I'm asking Jesus for someone who'll guide me through the pitfalls of crafting my first creative work. Like He sent Dash to Lily, so she could write *The Children's Hour*."

"Lillian Hellman was Jewish," said Mother.

"Then I'll ask Jehovah," I said.

"Lillian Hellman looked like my elbow," she said.

"Mother. You're not playing."

"I'm beginning to think the power of prayer works better in getting rid of people you don't want than in bringing people you do."

To be honest, this thought had also crossed my mind. I'd pleaded with Jesus to fling Eddie, Mother's hideous church girlfriend, from our lives, and He had. After Mother's first weekend in Lubbock with Mr. Taft, she'd stopped returning Eddie's phone calls. "Men are too much work," she'd said. "But women are *really* too much work." And at that moment, I'd truly felt the Lord's presence in my life. On the other hand, praying had yet to score me any romantic leads, particularly in the form of left-wing mystery writers. "What kind of husband do you want?" I asked.

"Dead," she said.

"If a man dropped out of the sky? Who would he be?"

"I don't know," said Mother. She scraped a little smidge of ash off the tip of her tongue with her fingernail.

"Sure you do," I said.

"I don't want to discuss him with you," she said.

And that's when I knew my days with Mother were numbered.

CHAPTER NINE

A Woman Who Arranges Things

If the reason I followed the advice of Mrs. Rayburn, my perhaps-evil high school geometry teacher, and auditioned for the starring role of Tony in the Northwest Houston Community Playhouse's Christmas production of *West Side Story* was to escape the drearier aspects of my life, then I hadn't chosen the obvious spot for whimsy. The theater was a converted warehouse in a suburban industrial complex. It looked like *Panic in Needle Park*, and when the monsoon rains of Houston collided with its corrugated tin roof, the racket, which was not unlike being cluster bombed, rung the curtain down. The phrase "rung the curtain down" being, here, metaphorical, since the Northwest Houston Community Playhouse didn't even have a curtain. What it had was a light switch, operated by a gnomish old lady whose nervous ailment caused her face to ball into violent blinking spasms once every three Mississippis. Sometimes, while she held the spotlight, the blare of its lamp would trigger a catatonic state, and as she sat spellbound, the spot would slowly veer onto the ceiling. In general, it was shocking how the lure of a stage, any stage, drew the lunatic fringe out from their places of hiding.

Not that the Playhouse didn't also attract housewives, and after-work career gals, and former drama club types—frothy, chattering women who crowded the chorus. But the lone reason Tina Marie, our impresario, cast me as Tony was because, of the dozens who'd tried out, I was the only halfway normal young man who could carry a tune, and wasn't so ugly I had to slip up on the dipper (as the O'Dooles would say). Still, I managed to believe I'd been chosen by Tina because she recognized something of herself in me. For, if I'd arrived at the Northwest Houston Community Playhouse looking for whimsy, I stayed because of Tina Marie.

Anyone could tell Tina was a star. But in case they missed it, she drew tiny five-point stars over the lowercase "i"s in her signature. She glued rhinestones onto her sunglasses, and cruised Houston in her Zimmer—a long, gilt-trimmed roadster like Cruella De Vil's. Black marble stars were laid into the floors of Tina's house, and several times she'd been forcibly ejected by the late-night management of the local Denny's for belting out, over pancake suppers, her signature song: "I Just Want to Be a Star!"

Unlike those eager ladies of the Playhouse chorus, Tina deserved every last rhinestone. In the 1960s, the last moment it meant a damn, she'd been a Broadway star. Tina Marie: beat Streisand out of chorus parts; danced in *Roar of the Greasepaint, Smell of the Crowd;* headlined *A Lady*

Named Jo (a musical of *Little Women*); and led so many touring productions of *Mame* and *Gypsy* and *Hello, Dolly!* and *The Unsinkable Molly Brown* that, by the time I knew her, she'd absorbed *the* lesson of musical comedy—that imagination creates the greatest reality—into a persona that was difficult to exaggerate.

Rehearsals for *West Side Story* began in October. And in less than a month, I was barnacle-attached to Tina, having joined the circle of young devotees who jostled for her favor. Tina's attentions helped to wean me away from Mother, whose eye was on Mr. Taft. I couldn't help thinking of her as the version of Mother who'd managed to forge craft from personality. Tina was, after all, another mouthy woman who wore sunglasses indoors, and thought style (at least) as important as substance, and who also, interestingly enough, had been abandoned by her husband. If Tina turned a blind eye to the real world, it was probably because, show tunes aside, much of her life had been pretty depressing.

Tina landed in the Houston suburbs after marrying Dick, an affluent drapery manufacturer who demanded she give up the stage. When Tina stopped performing she gained five pounds. "Gain ten more," said Dick the Draper, "and I'll divorce you." Then Tina gained ten more, and Dick did. By the time she auditioned for Reno Sweeney in the Playhouse's *Anything Goes*, she'd gained another thirty. But the community theater celebrated Tina's bouncing figure—she gave the Playhouse a genuine star, and it gave her imagination a permanent venue. Tina made the Northwest Houston Community Playhouse into a place where it was difficult not to become somebody else, and the woman she became believed there was no such thing as too many ostrich feathers. "Reality is something you have to strive to overcome," she told me while rehearsing *West Side Story*. I thought this made her a genius, until I found out it was a line from a Liza Minnelli concert. This taught me two things about Tina: To her, the world really was a stage, and she didn't believe in giving credit to the writers.

One evening, after rehearsal, when I'd offered to help her lock up the darkened theater for the chance of hearing another of her New York stories, I confessed, "I've never heard of *A Lady Named Jo*."

"That's because it was lousy," Tina said, jangling through a fat ring of keys, searching for the one that would lock the side door.

"Bad music?" I asked.

"Bad story," she said.

"*Little Women?*" I asked.

"Borr-ingg!" said Tina, like a gong tolling. "I kept telling the guys, 'Guys,' I said, 'nobody cares about these characters.' And they kept giving me, 'But Tina, it's a classic.' And I kept saying, 'Maybe in 1865 it was a classic. But in 1965, it's boring.' Well, they stuck to the book. And we closed after forty-eight performances." Tina bolted the door.

No one would have accused Tina Marie of sticking too close to the book. She lived in flagrant violation of copyright law, because she didn't believe anything was so good it couldn't be improved upon. Her Playhouse shows, even the standards, were wild divergences. By the time she'd explained to me the ruin of *A Lady Named Jo,* most of the boring parts had already been cut from *West Side Story.* Along with the sad and the violent parts. This nipped the show down to about an hour. And the scenes that did survive were nearly unrecognizable. This was suburban Houston, there were no Puerto Ricans, or even Italians, in our cast, and the average member of our chorus was in his early forties. The Sharks and the Jets looked less like street gangs, and more like a Shriners' convention.

I'd been too tipsy with my own stardom to consider that, as Christmas musicals go, *West Side Story* was a real stretch. But that was before Tina added the carolers. In toppling stovepipe hats and bristling fur mufflers, with rosy red, cider-flushed cheeks, they carried holly branches and sang "We Need a Little Christmas Right This Very Minute" during the pre-show and entr'acts.

Tina Marie made each of her "improvements" with a flourish that was difficult to doubt—at least openly. I tended to accept her extravagances on faith. But when our production's Maria, a plump young woman who'd won her part by boasting a baked skin tone the color of a macaroon, contracted spinal meningitis, and was replaced by a frowsy alto whose husband was the swing vote needed to push *Call Me Madam,* Tina's proposed summer musical, through the Play Reading Committee, I mustered the daring to ask Tina if she didn't think my serenading a woman who challenged the very outer limits of middle age, and who looked not a little like my aunt Edie, seemed a bit odd. To which Tina asked me if I knew how to tap dance.

And when I said no, I didn't know how to tap dance,

and what's more, I couldn't, off the top of my head, recall any tapping being done in the filmed version of *West Side Story*, she said, "What about the Kansas City Shuffle?" And when I wondered aloud whether there might be *some* people who'd consider the dancing of the Kansas City Shuffle to "Gee, Officer Krupke" a compromise of our artistic integrity, Tina put her arm around my shoulder.

Like all the best despots, Tina had a little, electric body, like a bumblebee. She was about fourteen inches shorter than I was, and in order for her to put her arm around my shoulder, I had to sort of slump over to one side. "Back when I lived in New York," Tina said to me. She gestured as though conjuring an image of the past. "Back when I was a student of the famous Stella Adler," she said. "There were many young men. These young men were handsome, and they were talented, and they spent their days sitting in cafés talking of art. And you, Robert," said Tina. "You remind me of those young men."

"I do?" I asked. My voice was almost dewy.

"You do," said Tina. "They were also unemployed. Because no one ever hired them. Because all they wanted to do was sit around like bums all day talking about art. Do you understand what I'm trying to tell you?"

"That this production of *West Side Story* isn't art. That this is entertainment?" I asked.

"Wrong," said Tina. "This is community theater."

"This is a miasma," Mother said, sitting with *W* magazine in the back row of the Playhouse, as she often did on the days she wasn't off gallivanting with Mr. Taft. She'd just witnessed the mangling of a Swiss bell routine by certain chorus members during a first-act run-through. "Are you really this desperate for attention, Robert?"

"My life is the theater," I said, tormenting Mother because I felt she could be nicer.

"You're dancing in a warehouse with a bunch of people who look like refugees," Mother said. To illustrate, she pointed her W towards Duane—a squat tippling sandbag of a man with a mullet who doubled in the chorus as a Santa Claus and a Jet. Duane did terrible things to a Swiss bell. He stank of liquor, and swayed under his own weight, and did, in fact, carry the unkempt, crazy-eyed look of someone applying for political asylum. Duane definitely qualified for the lunatic fringe. But Duane wasn't the person Mother was really gunning for; ultimately, she'd set her sights on a bigger target. "Tina Marie has you buffaloed. That's got to be the reason you're staying in this crummy show," she said. "God, I hate little people."

Mother was always making catty remarks about Tina; she'd had an absolute field day with the ostrich plumes. One evening, for instance, as we were making the long drive back to Petunia from the Houston suburbs, Mother gestured out the window towards a dead swan, white feathers akimbo, that had been plowed down in oncoming traffic after escaping from the scenic pond of a mid-priced apartment complex, and said, "Oh look, Tina dropped her handbag."

"I've never enjoyed anyone's company more than Tina Marie's," I said. I found Mother's jealousy galling. Especially since I'd only tried out for West Side Story because

I'd suspected I was handicapping her romance with Mr. Taft. Even still, she couldn't stand the idea of being replaced.

"Fine," Mother said. "But I'm warning you. Those goddamned bell ringers are going to steal this show right out from under you."

The first time Tina went an entire rehearsal without removing her sunglasses with the glue-on rhinestones, I couldn't wait to introduce her to Mother.

This, of course, had been a mistake.

Because there was something I'd yet to learn about women like Mother and Tina Marie, a lesson I would, in fact, spend years learning: They don't like each other.

Before their meeting, I'd attempted to assure the women of their similarities—an effort they both seemed to accept as a challenge. "Tina's also suffered through a very painful divorce," I said. "That's how she got stuck in Texas."

"Tragic," said Mother, barely glancing up from *Women's Wear Daily*.

"My mother," I told Tina, "is no stranger to the stage herself. Long before she was Cotton Bowl Princess and The Lester's Girl, she headlined her high school's *Oklahoma!*"

"Precious," said Tina, making notes on a fan dance she'd planned for "I Feel Pretty."

Finally, during a rehearsal break, Tina Marie indulged me by climbing the stairs to Mother's seat in the back row. "Tina Marie," I said, "this is my mother. And Mother," I said. "This is Tina Marie."

"How do you do," said Mother. Like she was Marie of Romania.

"I'm ever so fond of your son," said Tina. Like she was Ethel Barrymore.

"This town ain't big enough for the both of us" is what they both meant. And since I was the town, and this was the O.K. Corral all over again, I made a very unfunny joke about mothers and stages and nobody laughed. We were all relieved when Tina said she hoped we'd excuse her, as she had a fan dance to see to. "Were you adopted?" she asked me later that evening.

"Is Tina Marie blind?" Mother asked me as soon as Tina had walked away.

"Blind?" I said.

"I've just never seen her without sunglasses," Mother said. "Also, she's so musical. Those people seem prone to blindness. Like Little Stevie Wonder." Then, Mother lifted *Women's Wear Daily* so high it covered her face, and pretended to read an article about the wraparound skirt. And if Mother's own sunglasses hadn't been perched in her wig at the time, and if I hadn't known she'd only removed them in the first place because it gave her eye-strain headaches to read by the Playhouse's overhead lighting, I probably would have considered this mere mid-tier bitchiness, instead of a fascinating insight into why we never got the ERA ratified.

Mother's failure of self-perception was no greater than Tina's when it came to Stella Adler. One afternoon, I sat and watched Tina hand-feed her Malteses cubed chicken, and as those little dogs leapt on hind legs for their supper, grilled personally by Tina each day, she regaled me with snide anecdotes on Stella Adler's absurdity—which seemed to rest primarily on the fact that she had her hair streaked and fluffed and parted in the middle in order to match her Lhasa apsos. And while Tina's story was very amusing, I couldn't help but notice, as she taunted her lapdogs with chicken bits, how perfectly their tiny satin hair ribbons, dancing merrily in the light, coordinated with Tina's silk blouse, causing me to think hard about the power of Sisterhood and the insidiousness of the patriarchy.

Of course, the real pity was that Mother and Tina, even as they allowed feminist opportunity to pass them by, were powerful, political women. Though they kept their distance, and barely waved to each other across the theater, they certainly knew how to network when it came to handling me. Mother was Tina's natural ally when it came to getting me to spend extra time memorizing my lines or doing vocal exercises. And I don't think it was any coincidence that Tina waited for an evening when she knew Mother would be sitting in the back row, to ask another of her people, a young choreographer and student at the local state university, who'd played Jesus in her (highly apocryphal) production of *Godspell*, to coach my dancing, since I was a real washout when it came to the Kansas City Shuffle. I think Tina needed Mother to witness the moment I met Michael Leleux.

"Here's a young man for you to take under your wing," Tina said to Michael, who was so darkly French I found myself thinking he must shave twice a day to keep his olive skin so smooth.

"There's a lot you can learn from Michael," Tina told me, except I didn't hear because I was too distracted thinking how much the Brontë sisters would have loved Michael's broody, handsome face. He had almond-shaped eyes, which only seemed to darken in the light, and he could have cut diamonds with his jaw line. His leonine hair and broad chest seemed oversized, on the verge of lunging out from his small body. Just when I began to suspect he'd been born to wander the moors, Michael smiled, and shook my hand, and showed his dimples, which both revealed his furry, giggling personality, and spoiled any resemblance he bore to Mr. Rochester.

Years ago, I read a book I've now forgotten. And the only thing I remember about it is the mention of a Canadian who bruised her brain in a fall, and upon recovering, found herself fluent in French, a language she'd never spoken. That's what it felt like meeting Michael that Thursday evening at the Playhouse—I saw his almond eyes, which were, in point of fact, French, and I could already remember adoring him. It took enormous effort to look squarely into his face.

Mother had removed her sunglasses by the time Michael's dimples winked. She saw the dumb, lucky, animal expression overcome my face. Then, she plopped back into her folding chair. "Well," she said to herself. "That's that."

CHAPTER TEN

Jesus Hates a Vacuum

The air was crisp as hotel sheets on the blue, cool Sunday in November when Mother accepted Mr. Taft's proposal. Boarding the afternoon flight back to Houston from Lubbock, she caught with one hand—the hand laden with her square diamond engagement ring—the kisses blown by her new fiancé, as he stood in the terminal wearing a yellow golf shirt and his best toupée, and with her other hand—the one invisible and folded into her silver fox jacket that was really too warm for the weather—she clawed her tender palm to keep herself from sobbing. "My life is a torture," Mother said to herself, casting Mr. Taft a pining smile to say how much she'd miss him.

But as soon as Mr. Taft was out of sight, as soon as Mother had turned and walked onto the plane's ramp, she began to sob. For a while, the thrill of the bear hunt had spiked her adrenaline flow sufficiently to distract her from her loathing of Lubbock, of Mr. Taft's company, and of eating the eggs which were regularly foisted upon her for lunch at Mr. Taft's twenty-four-hour breakfast joints. But now that Mother's work had come to triumph, she was deluged with the depression that accompanies success. Mr. Taft had bought Mother a first-class ticket home, and in the easy gray leather of her seat, Mother pulled off her mules and tucked her stockinged feet beneath her. Then, using her jacket for a blanket, she leaned into the window and wailed.

Mother's first complimentary champagne flute, offered by a stewardess eager to hush her crying, did nothing to relax her. Her second and third champagnes were, likewise, of little effect. By the time Mother swilled her fourth flute, however, the sun was grinning softly through the window, and even though crying had left sharp pain, jagged as a broken fingernail, spreading across her forehead, the wide, endless plains of gray-brown prairie below seemed somehow dazzling and wonderful.

For a brief while, Mother dozed, as the sun glowed through her eyelids and dried the mucky tracks of mascara on her cheeks. When she awoke, she asked the stewardess for Tylenol, some napkins, and ice water. Mother swallowed the capsules with her last gulp of champagne; and dunking the napkins into the ice water until they made a cold, runny lump, she mopped her face with them. Then she reached into her makeup bag, and just as she began to recoat her false eyelashes with her mascara wand, she felt the eyes of the man in the seat beside her. Which she found peeving.

Until she turned and saw Peter's face.

When Mother turned and gazed at Peter's face, she couldn't see that its sheen and texture were precisely that of vinyl kitchen tile. And she couldn't see that Peter had suffered such overexposure to the sun (from boat racing and mountain climbing) that his flesh had begun to resemble an old paper bag somebody inflated, and then sat on. Mother failed to observe that Peter's shiny, tanned, weathered quality was that of a man whose life had been devoted to sexual conquest; that his sloe eyes and wavy, dark, Kennedy-esque hair conveyed the appearance of someone who, in his youth, had taken a Dark Journey and never come back. Most sadly, Mother missed the gentle caress with which Peter held his scotch and soda. And the reason Mother failed to notice that the man beside her belonged to that class of middle-aged swinger who considers a hot tub an aphrodisiac, and chose to see, instead, a handsome sophisticate whose teeth shone like klieg lights from his laugh-lined face, was because she'd fallen blindly in love with Peter.

But none of it would have mattered to Mother anyway. It wouldn't have mattered if she'd known, at the time, cuddled in her fox jacket, patting wrinkle-concealing foundation over her tear-stained face while flying home from Lubbock, that Peter actually subscribed to *USA Today* (which is a very fine newspaper if you happen to be a La Quinta Inn). Mother wouldn't have cared about Peter's mousy first wife divorcing him after discovering the string of assignations he'd made through anonymous-sex clubs.

Because rather than renting a P.O. box like any other nymphomaniacal degenerate, Peter had saved the fourteen-ninety-five, and given the glad rags their home address—because not only was he a pervert, he was a chinchy pervert. And even if Mother had been able to see everything I saw so clearly when I first met Peter years later, long after she'd packed a single overnight case and left her life forever to move into his California stag pad, she would have married him or died.

Peter had been seated in the aisle seat next to Mother since several minutes before their departure from Lubbock, and yet she hadn't noticed him until just that moment. Afterward, however, Mother wasted no time in establishing the pertinent facts of Peter's financial status—he designed airplanes, had made a killing in real estate, and owned houses in Sausalito, Lake Tahoe, and Key West. Once satisfied, Mother tucked her left hand under her jacket, and slipped Mr. Taft's engagement ring into her satin-lined pocket, and then she flitted that hand in the air, oohing and laughing at every brilliant, hilarious word that dropped from Peter's sun-parched, craggy lips in his unmistakably military baritone (Peter was a retired lieutenant colonel in the air force). So by the time the plane's wheels touched ground in Houston, Mother's engagement to Mr. Taft was as good as over, and her marriage to Peter as good as begun.

When I picked Mother up that evening, under the carport of the Houston Intercontinental Airport, she'd already stopped at a baggage claim pay phone and ended things with Mr. Taft. Walking toward the car, Mother looked dazed. She seemed to be repeating a conversation to herself, mouthing words and shaking her head back and forth. At first, she didn't see me waving, and after she'd pitched her overnight case into the trunk and plopped into the passenger's seat, she didn't respond to my hello. In the low bucket seat, Mother's collar rose, and hid the bottom half of her face in long fox fur. "So?" I asked. "How'd things go with Mr. Taft?"

"I told him I had syphilis," Mother said.

I put my hand on top of Mother's hand and squeezed, and while squeezing, almost ran the car off the airport road and into the WELCOME TO HOUSTON sign next to the Flags of All Nations light sculpture. "Oh, Mother," I said. "Oh, Mother, do you?" I should have known better, because Mother had apparently spent her youth warding off the advances of Texas A&M football players with the threat of syphilis. If a boy got grabby at a party, then Mother had syphilis. If she found herself in a darkened convertible with a signal-light blinking away from her dorm room, then Mother suddenly contracted syphilis. "It sounds worse than herpes, or gonorrhea, even. Not even a date-rapist wants to play it fast and loose with syphilis, Robert," Mother said. But Mother looked so strange, so bewildered and shaken on that November evening I picked her up from the airport, that I thought, this time, Mother really might have VD.

"Well, of course I don't have syphilis, Robert. Good God."

I stopped squeezing Mother's hand. "Then what are you talking about?"

Mother shook her head, and rubbed her hands over her trouser legs. "Mr. Taft proposed," she said in a hushed, carved-out voice. "We were just about to order lunch— more goddamned eggs. And he said, 'What would you like?' And I said, 'Scrambled,' like always. And he said, 'Anything else?' And I said, 'Maybe a corn muffin.' And he said, 'Why not something different?' And I said, 'You mean like over-easy?' And he said, 'Like marrying me.' And then, he slid this ring across the table." Mother took the ring out of her pocket, and held it out in front of her. "It was in one of those little velvet boxes. But I don't have it anymore because there was some grape jelly on the table, and when Mr. Taft slid it over to me, it got all sticky, so he started hollering at the busboy about cleaning the tables better. And then he said, 'So?' And all I wanted to say was that I'd rather have scrambled eggs. But what I really said was, 'You've made me the happiest woman in the world.' And then I started crying. Partly in order to look like the happiest woman in the world, but mostly because this was the best my life had to offer me: scrambled eggs." Mother tossed her engagement ring into the car's ashtray.

"Then what happened?" I asked.

"Then our food came; so we ate. Mr. Taft really doesn't let anything interfere with meals."

"But I don't understand. How'd you get from lunch to syphilis?"

"Well, after lunch, Mr. Taft took me shopping, and then he drove me to the airport to say good-bye. And I started crying on the plane, thinking about my life being a torture, and how much I didn't want to marry Mr. Taft, and then I tried to fix up my face with some wet napkins that this bitch stewardess brought me, and then I met a man."

"I don't follow," I said.

"There was this man named Peter. He was sitting next to me in first class. He looks kind of like JFK, and sort of like Steve McQueen, and a bit like Warren Beatty. Actually, he looks a lot like Steve McQueen and nothing like Warren Beatty, but he has a certain Warren Beatty quality, if you know what I mean." Mother was now talking very fast, but her voice still sounded hollow and flat.

"I don't know what you mean."

"Well, when you meet him you'll know. Anyway, this man started talking to me. Oh, he's had the most exciting life. Nothing at all like your father or Mr. Taft. He flew bombers in Vietnam, like in *Apocalypse Now*. And he was almost an astronaut! He made it down to the very final round at NASA before they cut him. But he got to meet Buzz Aldrin, Robert!" When Mother spoke of Peter being an almost-astronaut, she began showing signs of excitement, and by the time she got to Buzz Aldrin, *she* was practically buzzing. "And now he designs airplanes. Which is why he was in Lubbock—to supervise a test flight. Except he doesn't work so much now, he mainly just spends his time yachting and skiing and rock-climbing all over the world. And he gave me his phone number, Robert!" Mother drew a crumpled napkin out of the same jacket pocket that had held Mr. Taft's engagement ring, and ran her finger over Peter's name. Then, almost in a whisper, Mother said, "Then I gave him my phone number. And he said he hoped I'd come visit him in California sometime."

"What kind of masher asks a strange woman on an airplane to come stay with him in California?" I asked.

"Well," said Mother. She'd turned away, and was staring out the window. "I was really thinking that I might like to go. You know how I love California."

"You said California was The Land of Fruits and Nuts," I said.

"I did not," said Mother. "That was your father, I'm sure. *I've* always adored California."

"What about Mr. Taft?"

"Oh, that's handled. I called him from baggage claim, and said that as much as it broke my heart, I couldn't become his wife because I have syphilis."

"And he believed you?"

"Not at first. First, he asked me how I caught it, and I said your father brought it home from his little jockey whore. And then he got really frightened, and asked why I hadn't mentioned this earlier. So I said it was because I thought the penicillin took. Only now I knew it hadn't, and who knows, it might never, and I was really very sorry, but under these circumstances we could never marry."

"Well, I can't believe this," I said. "I mean, all this time, you've been desperate to marry Mr. Taft. Then, as soon as he proposes, you invent a social disease on account of some wolf you met on an airplane? What are you, in love with this guy?"

"I don't know," said Mother. "I can't make any sense out of it myself. Maybe it's just the champagne I drank on the plane. Or the relief of knowing I never, ever have to eat another goddamned egg again for the rest of my life."

I should have been more considerate of Mother's predicament. Since it took me a little under twelve minutes to fall in love with Michael, I, of all people, should have understood the brain trauma that results from falling in love with a stranger; the effort of fitting words to an experience that seems profound, but sounds silly or crazy. But I didn't feel like being understanding. I found the situation infuriating. It seemed to me that the behavior of a forty-five-year-old woman should be held to a higher, and somewhat less erratic, standard than that of her seventeen-year-old son. It was embarrassing, it seemed stagy and undignified, the way our lives turned, so drastically, on a moment's notice—the way Daddy left us for Pam, and I met Michael, and Mother met Peter. It seemed so unlike real life, unlike the slow, boring, quotidian pace I'd heard normal people describe when talking about their lives. Even at seventeen, I'd run into them at the post office, those normal people, and I'd ask them, "What's new?" and they'd say, "Nothing," and they weren't being polite. Nothing had changed for them, good or bad: They worked the same jobs; were married to the same drab people; lived in the same dreary little houses. And looking at them, I'd know that, when we next met in the post office five years later, nothing *still* would have happened. When nothing happened to Mother and me, even in those years before Daddy left, and we'd been stuck on Nana and Papa's ranch, there was always *something*. Often wonderful things—like a month in Italy, or Daddy almost dying in a truck fire. Lately, however, there'd been too much change. I was grateful to Jesus for meeting Michael, and Mother was clearly thrilled about Peter, but enough was enough. I needed peace.

Also, since Mother's approach to romance had been careerist, and her remarriage carried considerable financial repercussions for both our lives, then, from a bird-in-the-hand perspective, poky Mr. Taft seemed a sounder venture than some leering, ten-cent jet-setter who may or may not have known Buzz Aldrin. Mother was just begging for heartbreak, begging to spend her last days in some walk-up apartment with a courtyard pool. Though I managed to exercise restraint and hold my tongue regarding all of these objections, I couldn't help but mention that the whole situation just seemed really tacky to me. Before Mr. Taft, I'd never even heard of anybody flying from Lubbock to Houston. I didn't even know a dinky town like Lubbock had an airport. "There's something so vulgar about falling in love with a man on public transportation," I told Mother.

"Well, it *was* first class, Robert," said Mother, rather weakly. "It's not as though I met him on the Metro bus." She was staring out the window again.

"Cabin assignment really has very little to do with the point I'm making," I said.

"Why is it, do you think," Mother asked, "that the ugliest part of Houston is the first part you see when you leave the airport?" Mother was looking at the rows of grimy, ramshackle buildings that lined the freeway from the airport, buildings set crazily down in pastures full of weeds. "It's not like that in other places—in Los Angeles, for instance. Why doesn't the mayor's office have all this knocked down? Plant wildflowers, or something? Where's Lady Bird Johnson when you fucking need her? That's what I'd like to know." Mother's voice seemed absent and dreamy, as if she was imagining the pastures springing with bluebonnets and primroses and Indian paintbrushes.

But I knew Mother wasn't dreaming about bluebonnets. What she was dreaming about was California.

CHAPTER ELEVEN

The Miracle Worker

Wing-work was foremost among Tina Marie's dramatic exercises—her own invention, it involved gliding across stage while daintily flapping imaginary angels' wings as though preparing to make the Ascension. As a warmup, wing-work was supposed to make you nimble. But it crossed my mind, when Michael Leleux told me he'd lived in New York, that Thursday evening I met him in dance rehearsal—when romance, as unwieldy as a Wurlitzer, thumped between us, and Mother beamed knowingly from the back row—that all my wing-work had been rewarded with a miracle. "In Manhattan?" I asked him.

"In Chelsea," he answered. And if this had been a movie, I would have heard a waltz.

Then Michael made the dreadful mistake of carrying on. "I just moved back here a few months ago," he said. "I wanted to dance. But I couldn't stand living so far from home. I got lonesome for Texas. And most of all, I missed seeing my family. I'm sure you understand." He nodded toward my mother.

Granted, not a miracle as in Loaves and Fishes, I thought to myself. But then, nobody looks like that and cures cancer on the side. And since I could honestly say that *not* seeing my family was the bright side of my parents' divorce, and because, unless you're a royal, family seems to be the consolation prize for people who can't manage to surround themselves with better people, the only reason I could think of that anybody would choose to come back home was abject stupidity. "You must have *some* family, is all I can say," I said. Which was a lie, because truly there was much more I could say.

"My mother would love you," Michael said.

"Do you really think so?" I said. "How long did you say you lived in New York?"

"This time?" asked Michael.

"*This* time," I said.

"Well, let's see," said Michael, screwing up his gorgeous face. "The first time was right after I graduated from high school, because I'd won this huge scholarship. That time I stayed almost a month. Then I went back a couple of years later, and stayed nearly three weeks. But this time, this time I lasted just under a year."

It must have been the dimples that saved him. Because at that very moment, the tiny launched boat of our love might have gurgled and sunk if Michael's good looks had reminded me even slightly less of a Tibetan butter sculpture in their exquisite wastefulness. Every time that man passes a mirror, I thought, he ought to thank the ever-loving Lord.

"When would you like your first lesson?" Michael asked. It had been quickly established in the first few minutes of rehearsal—as I tried, really tried, to sway with the beat, while also contemplating the potential romantic tragedy of having fallen in love at first glance with a dancer, which was an irony worthy of *West Side Story*—that I was in desperate need of dancing lessons.

I leveled with Michael, before he even pushed the PLAY button on the rehearsal tape of "Gee, Officer Krupke," about my life-record of failure in physical education. I relayed the sad tale of my aerobics instructor claiming there was no class on the day he shot his fitness video. And that I'd overheard the golf pro at the country club telling Mother he felt guilt-stricken cashing her checks.

But then Michael put his hand on my waist, which felt like somebody dropped the radio into the bathtub. "Just relax, Robert," he told me. "I've led workshops for the disabled."

"In an hour, you'll be very sorry you told me that," I said.

"If that's true," he replied, "then I promise to make you my personal challenge." Then color spots blotted my eyes, as he grabbed my pant leg and pulled my foot into position.

"Oh, please don't say that," I said. "That's what Gene Kelly said in every movie to every person who ended up dancing alongside him. And I swear, that's not how this story goes. In this story, I'm Helen Keller and you're Annie Sullivan and we're a long, long way from pumping water at the well."

Michael gave me that look the Mexican waiter gives you when you try to order in Spanish. Then he made the shushing sign and pushed PLAY, and for whatever thoughts he maintained about my false modesty, I'm not to be blamed. For the next hour, Michael was breathless because of my utter inability to translate thought into deed and I was breathless because the chest hair peeking out of Michael's T-shirt looked like the enchanted forests in fairy tales. This time, he was the one seeing spots, but for no reason even remotely flattering. Finally, after rewinding the rehearsal tape perhaps a half-dozen times, Michael put his hands on his knees and blinked up at the ceiling and said, "I think . . . I think you might be a candidate for private lessons."

At once it occurred to me that there might after all be an advantage to fish-flopping before the man on earth to whom I most wished to appear attractive. "Lessons with you?" I asked.

Never had humiliation been so worthwhile.

"Of course with me," he wheezed. He'd yet to recover his breath.

"Only they couldn't be very expensive," I said. Because at that point, Mother and I were alternating weekly between shampoo and conditioner.

"Don't worry about the money," said Michael.

"Did you hear that, Mother?" I called out to her in the back. "Michael's going to teach me to dance, and he says not to worry about the money."

"Every word," Mother said.

At that moment, I gazed at Michael, who seemed so perfect, and I wondered why I hadn't noticed it before, that there was something of Dashiell Hammett around his eyes. Then Michael smiled at me, and, again, if this had been a movie, his white teeth would have sparkled and dinged in his dark face. "Where does somebody like you come from?" I asked him.

Which is when Michael mentioned New York and my thoughts moved towards the miraculous, and then he mentioned his family, which sent me careening back down to earth. "Right," I said. "My first lesson."

"How's a week from Saturday sound?" Michael asked.

A week from Saturday sounded just fine. Mother was (already!) jetting off for California to visit Peter, so I'd have her car. "Where do you teach?" I asked. "A school? A studio? An atelier?"

"In my mother's living room," said Michael.

God was slapping my hand for the atelier bit. "How old are you?" I asked.

"Twenty-five," said Michael.

"Hmmm," I said. "Tina told me you're in college."

"I commute to college," said Michael. "But I live with my parents."

Beauty sure isn't everything, I thought.

"What time?" asked Michael.

"What time," I said. "What time a week from Saturday am I coming to your mother's house so we can dance around her living room." I was a weathervane and fate was the wind.

Then Michael made that bothersome, bucking gesture people make when their luscious, scintillating hair is so thick and luxurious it tickles their eyes. "Seven-thirty," Mother shouted from the back row.

At some point in the evening, the thought crossed my mind that if I'd fallen instantaneously in love with Michael Leleux, then it must mean I was gay. But I don't want to overstate this, because as eurekas go, it was fairly low-key, and also because it seemed so utterly beside the point, and not particularly interesting—since Michael and his dimples were the point, and getting to spend as much time with all three of them was what I found interesting. But if realizing I was gay was kind of like nothing at all—"Kind of like having a mother and a father," as Sarah Churchill used to say—it was also kind of like those movies where a young person is suddenly told she's a member of the Russian aristocracy and in response asks, "Is that why we have all those samovars in the garage?" By which I mean it was the ultimate frame of reference through which to view the rest of my life— providing useful insights, for instance, into why I found myself the only young man from Trinity Lutheran High School spending his evenings in *West Side Story*, as well as into the particular relationship I shared with my mother.

"Mother," I waited several weeks to say, "I have an announcement to make."

"I'm listening," said Mother. She'd reached the sheared-cat phase of removing her makeup.

"Mother," I said, steeling myself with a lace pillow. "Mother, I have fallen in love with Michael Leleux, which also means I'm gay."

"With Michael *Luuuluuuu*?" asked Mother. Cold cream oozed through her fingers.

"*Leleux*," I said. "Try making a tulip with your mouth."

"Spell it for me," Mother said. "Start with 'L.' "

"Mother," I said. "There's forests and then there's trees."

"I apologize," she said. "It comes as no surprise to me that you've fallen in love with Michael *Luuuluuuu*."

"You mean you've known about my feelings for Michael?"

"Since you first laid eyes on him," she said.

"And that I'm gay?" I asked.

"Since I first laid eyes on you," she said.

"And nothing about this catches you unawares?" I asked. Because, honestly, I found Mother's response a tad bit lackluster.

"*Unawares*, Robert?" she said. "Look at me." Mother's real hair floated like she was underwater. The way her eyeliner was smeared looked like she'd seen musket fire. "How could you be my child and *not* be gay? Women like me *always* have gay children. Cher, Lana Turner, Queen Elizabeth. My God, look at Queen Elizabeth."

"Mother," I groaned. "How did you become the subject of this conversation?"

"Come closer," she said.

"How did the private details of my love life make you into a star?" I said.

Mother put her arm around me. I felt something wet and goopy against my shoulder. "Because, Robert," she said, "I will always be the only woman in your life. Because, Robert, I adore you."

I exhaled so that my lips fluttered, and laid my head on top of Mother's head. "You know," I told her, "you could have told me this before."

"No," she said, "I couldn't have."

"Oh, Mother," I said. "About Michael. He's a . . . family man."

Mother shook my head away, and grabbed a moist towelette to wipe her fingers clean. "Yeah," she said. "Tell me all about it."

Sometime that fall, I dreamed I was a guest on the *Barbara Walters Special*. Barbara kept asking me questions about my life and I kept telling stories about Mother, until finally Barbara said, "You're under the impression that the story of your life is your mother's story. But in time you'll realize that the story of your life is your own." Which is one good reason not to watch too much TV, because the story of my life *is* my mother's story. It's even worse than Rilke said—we don't just dance to the unlived lives of our parents, we dance to the ones they did live, too. My mother wasted her youth with a stay-at-home husband. And at the first available opportunity, what did I do? I fell in love, first-off and finally, with a man who hadn't just stayed home, but who kept coming back after having been given every reasonable chance to escape. All

I'd ever dreamed of was parlaying myself to New York or Paris, and living a life as unlike the O'Dooles' as possible. But Michael was like those life-term inmates who finally get paroled, then knock over a convenience store because they get nostalgic for prison. And I'd fallen for the guy! Which altogether made me no better than those women in the tabloids who marry convicts and knock themselves up with a turkey baster. And had anybody asked me, I'd have told them just what those women always say: that I loved Michael and I had no choice. Even though I'd been raised on the free-will doctrine! Not to mention eight shows a week of *Moscow!Moscow!*, Mother's own one-woman musical version of *The Three Sisters*.

But "from the very first moment I beheld him, my heart was irrevocably gone." Jane Austen wrote that in *Northanger Abbey*, only she was joking. But I bought a frame with that printed on it, and I put Michael's picture in it. And while I really am bourgeois and dippy enough to blame dimples and kismet and the Brontë of your choice, and believe I'd have toppled for Michael Leleux under whichever star I happened to be born, I nevertheless prefer to blame my mother for my particular star. Because in terms of generational karma, I believe that if Mother had made nice with her in-laws, then Michael and I could have begun on a blank page. If she'd managed to make peace with the dim, plain Republican values of her husband's family, then when I met Michael, maybe he'd have been raring and ready to go, and I wouldn't have had to hop from the frying pan of the O'Dooles' Irish, Baptist clannishness, and into the fire of the Leleuxs' Cajun-French,

Catholic variety. Maybe Michael and I could have started one step closer to enlightenment.

But as it happened, I couldn't even wait a week to start up with Michael. So when he mentioned, on that Thursday night we met, that the reason we couldn't begin our dance lessons right away—the reason we had to wait one unbearable, lingering week for me to be able to mortify myself prancing about his mother's living room—was because this Saturday he was flying away *to New York* (which just had to be a sign from God) for the weekend. I asked him what time his plane was leaving. "About two-thirty," Michael said.

I went home and called one airline after the next, until I finally found the only plane leaving Houston for New York at about two-thirty on Saturday, and then I spent Friday and my last nickel, too, shopping for whatever a person might want on a flight to New York—Malamars and magazines, a *Marlene Dietrich in London* tape—and by the time Michael arrived at the terminal that sparkling Saturday afternoon, I was standing there waiting for him, with my head tucked and grinning.

Michael had to look twice to believe it was me. "You're *not* coming with me?" he asked.

"Nope," I said.

"You came all the way out here just to say good-bye?"

"I'm not saying good-bye," I said.

Michael nodded his head, and I handed him his gift bag, which, when all was said and done, weighed about thirty-five pounds.

"I'm saying hello," I said.

Half of Michael's face smiled, so that his right eye was almost winking. His knees buckled slightly from the weight of the bag. "I really am coming back day after tomorrow," he said.

"I'll see you in a week," I said as Michael hitched his gift bag into his arms, and walked to the gate, and at least by the end of the weekend, and definitely by seven-thirty, the second Saturday after we first met, in the living room of 4315 Pebble Springs Drive, the Leleuxs' broad family house, which was built in the sixties to seem like it had stood forever behind one pine and one magnolia tree, and was as English Tudor as anyplace in suburban Houston, Michael Leleux had already fallen in love with me.

CHAPTER TWELVE

A Mother Knows

Since life for the whole clattering Leleux clan happened first in the kitchen, and then in the family room, the fact that Yvella Leleux surrendered her parlor to her only son when he moved, once again, home from Manhattan, was less of a sacrifice than it sounded. Mom (and *everybody* called her Mom) had made a long career of The Love That Endures All Things. After all, she'd married Chester Leleux when she was fourteen years old, in a time and place (Gueydan, Louisiana; the 1940s) when that practically made her a spinster. For the next forty-odd years, she and her husband and their mutual standards fought a doomed battle against their children's wants and capers. By Michael's last return home, Mom and Dad spent days in their bathrobes, and were too worn-out to care if he turned their living room into a shag-carpeted studio of theater and dance.

Behind the French doors of that studio, on that Saturday evening at seven-thirty, Michael gave me what we called a private dance lesson, even though very little dancing was done. Michael and I had slipped so fast from effort and industry into stuttery talk and dumb, doe-eyed staring that I found it nearly impossible to control my limbs. And even Michael, who specializes in a sort of Lion's Grit that can make you wish you were never born when it comes to choosing between toothpastes at the grocery store, began quickly to despair of my hopes as a dancer: "I'm not saying you'll never, as long as you live, be able to dance," he said. "What I'm saying is you're going to need a lot of lessons." Which was mighty fine by me: I didn't care if I never went home.

And in a manner of speaking, I never did.

Because in a way completely unlike real life, and even most decent fiction, Michael and I seamed together and stuck for good. One November evening, I arrived at the suburban home of Yvella and Chester Leleux, and I never left. Whether they knew it or not at the time (and I suspect they both knew it and not, but no matter what, they deserve a medal), I was a Kaufman & Hart play for the nineties: *The Son-in-Law Who Came to Dinner*. Which is probably a feature of my genetic fiber—because in the same manner of speaking, Mother flew away to California and never came back.

When Michael and I finally stumbled out of his studio, looking at each other like we'd discovered one of the lost tribes of Israel, he took my hand and led me into the family room. I would have followed him anywhere, and especially into a room that held the chance of meeting his parents. Even into the *family* room, which looked even more like a Knights of Columbus Hall than the rest of the house. It's not that the house wasn't lovely (particularly from the outside)—it reclined from the street like a big Tudor BarcaLounger and the bedrooms were practically suites. It's just that ever since Dad's stroke forced him to retire early from a stunning career at Pennzoil (considering his parents were, I swear to God, illiterate sharecroppers), there was only enough money to maintain the inside of the house or the outside of the house, and Dad chose the outside. On the inside, Mom kept what little furniture there was fizzing with Lemon Pledge, and achieved a nirvana of cleanliness with the walls and floors of which WASPs are simply not capable. But most of the Leleuxs' furniture had snapped like arthritic hips beneath the family's collective weight, and what remained seemed to have been permanently cast with impressions of their backsides. All the carpeting was shag and yarny, and ranged from Celery Green to Harvest Gold, and the family room was paneled in that plasticky walnut-colored veneer that suggests fishing lures or recreation centers like, as I've mentioned, the Knights of Columbus Hall. A resemblance strengthened by enough mournful Marys and dangling Jesuses and tiny flickering candles to snatch an entire heathen race from the jaws of perdition—not to mention being filled unto brimming with actual Catholics.

I cowered in the doorway. "Who are all these people?" I asked Michael.

"This," he smiled, "is my family."

"But am I interrupting something? A party, or something?"

Michael looked genuinely confused. "No," he said. "This is, you know, Saturday night. My sisters just dropped by with some of their kids."

"*Some* of their kids," I said.

Now, I can't write too much about Michael's sisters without getting a divorce, or at least before Mom, how shall we say, schedules the Full Day of Beauty at Elizabeth Arden. But what I can say is that some of Michael's sisters have children like they're trying to preserve the Grimaldi throne. Others share a certain myopic relationship to food that's flowed through their lily-French blood since Caesar conquered Gaul and makes extremely understandable those articles you're always reading about how the French countryside is rioting over the pasteurization of cheese. Even though, at that moment, Michael was the only Leleux child who happened to be living at 4315 Pebble Springs Drive (and the number of residents in that house fluctuated at a rate similar to the family's blood sugar levels), the family room was still flush with people, and operated on a level of noise I'd previously associated only with slaughterhouses.

A cartoon blazed from the TV set, as a cabal of wee, shrieking Catholics careened across the floor in lethal, wheeling toys. One of Michael's splendid-looking sisters was yelling into the telephone about the *real* difference between creamy and crunchy peanut butter, and eating a chicken leg, which, from the way she ripped the meat from the bone with her marvelous white teeth, had evidently committed some gross trespass against a dearly departed loved one. Another smashing sister burped a baby in a glider rocker—a kind of chair designed for the parents of newborn children, and which was a permanent fixture in the Leleux household. "Come on," said Michael. "I want you to meet Mom and Dad."

Michael's parents were sitting on a sofa that was, in its own dismal way, as plasticky as the paneling, and so sticky that it made vulgar toot-toot-tooting noises when you tried to cross your legs. Both wore velour bathrobes—except that in his, Dad looked bleak and mopey-eyed, while in hers, Mom was so darkly French and dimply gorgeous that she made purple velour look like a regal robe of state. I looked back and forth from Mom's face to Michael's, and then into the face of yet another of Michael's exquisite sisters—who was sucking icing off her fingers in such a way that I became concerned for the integrity of her fingerprints. Which reminded me of that old Redd Foxx joke about how if you follow an ugly kid home, and you ring the doorbell, chances are an ugly person will answer. Except in Michael's case, a beautiful person would answer—since in his family beauty seemed common as dirt. And as far as the velour could tell me, nearly as valuable—which was shocking, since Mother had based my childhood teachings on the premise that beauty traded on the free market with the rough value of plutonium. What a waste of natural resources, I thought. Like sitting on a diamond mine, I was thinking, when Michael interrupted Mom, who was telling Dad a story, in order to make our introductions. "Robert," said Michael. "I want you to meet my mother."

"Call me Mom," said Mom.

"And my father," said Michael.

"Hmmph," said Dad. Who really was a world-class grump.

"Mom and Dad," said Michael. "This is Robert O'Doole."

And this is the story Mom was telling before Michael interrupted her: ". . . you know, the black lady who used to make the lemon angel food cakes at the bakery. Her. Yes, her. Well, she told me she'd just gotten back from her daughter's graduation. And I said, 'From college?' And she said, 'You could say that.' And I said, 'What would you say?' And she said, 'Well, I'd say mortuary school. My girl has become an embalmer.' And I said, 'My Lord, what-ever made your daughter run off and become an em-balmer?' And she said, 'Do you know, Mrs. Leleux, it is her life's dream. Embalming's all she's ever, in her whole life, wanted to do.'

"But this is the weird part. Then the mother, the cake lady, she told me that ever since her daughter was a little girl, even before she could stand by herself and walk around, she used to look down into her playpen and say to herself, 'Something just tells me that this little girl's going to grow up to become an undertaker. You know how a mother knows.' And I looked right into her face, and I said to her, 'Yes, ma'am, that's sure right. A mother always knows.' "

Then Yvella Leleux, for the first time, looked right into my face and said, "Call me Mom."

This is how change occurs in big families: Michael's older sisters suffered.

They went to bed early, and never got to see the Johnny Carson show.

It was Fish on Fridays, even at sleepovers.

Saturday mornings were for cleaning house, and nobody cared that's when the Brownies met.

For sex education, they were shown a book with pen-and-ink sketches of cats and a bewildering series of phrases, written in Latin.

Then the first daughter married a French boy with an Afro who played the air-drums. Then the second daughter a Presbyterian divorcé with a motorcycle. Then the third daughter didn't marry, but had a baby with a man who was Assembly of God. So by the time Michael brought me home, Mom and Dad's resistance had worn so thin that Mom had given up entirely, and Dad eyed me with more or less the same disapproval as the Presbyterian, which was a moral system I could cope with.

But that's ungrateful—because the only real reason Yvella and Chester Leleux found their hearts hauled further, and then further, away from any terrain they recognized wasn't exhaustion. It was because they loved their children, and their children's happiness, and the spirit of their church more than its laws. And also because they had that crazed, Catholic mania for family that got Kennedy elected—where it didn't matter how you felt about the other person, because family wasn't a matter of feeling. It was a matter of principle: The Union Must Be Preserved.

Having married at fourteen, Mom came to love her husband in the way most people do their grandmother's china—Dad was precious and final, but not necessarily what she would have chosen. In a perfect world, neither was I. But then, Mom wasn't much on complicating a situation with thoughts of a perfect world. So when I was delivered like a parcel into her life, Yvella Leleux didn't worry that I wasn't Catholic or French; or that I was a man, and, at seventeen, a very young man at that. What concerned Mom was that, while I adored my mother (who was *unusual*, and hadn't spoken to her own parents in years), I hated my philandering father. I was engaged in a mental debate, throughout the early winter of 1996, as to which cartoon superpower I'd most like to possess for the purpose of brutally slaying Daddy and his mannish mistress.

"You don't really want to murder your father," said Mom. She shook her head like someone forgot to sugar her coffee. The concept of irony didn't exist in Michael's family, so they tended to find the gallows humor Mother and I preferred more terrifying than funny.

"It was only a joke," I said. Michael was in his studio, and there was no hope of reinforcements.

"But murdering your father isn't a joke," said Mom. She had a deep, soothing Gordon MacRae voice, perfect for coaxing kittens out of trees. Mom was sitting at the breakfast table snapping beans into a spaghetti strainer.

Whenever Mom lectured, she was always snapping beans. Or knitting booties. Or tatting. Or whatever other unimpeachable domestic chore was intended that afternoon to convey maternal authority. Once I had a doctor, and every time I went into his office he was chewing his pipe, or cleaning his pipe, or polishing his pipe, or fingering his pipe, but he was never, ever smoking it. Because here's what I think—I think the pipe was a prop. I don't think he'd even ever lit the damn thing. I think it was merely a paternalistic ruse to garner credibility. It was sneaky politics, and I thought about it every time Mom pled family unity and just happened to be putting up jelly. "I always thought a joke was something you did to make other people happy," said Mom.

"All I meant to say is that I hate my father," I explained. "That's all. And when I say that I long for the raw, electric power to cause human heads to explode merely by glancing at them, that's just a figure of speech."

"But he's your father," said Mom. Who tended to state the obvious in the form of wisdom.

"Yes, that's the problem," I said.

Mom sighed and snapped, "You only get one father, Robert."

"That's plenty," I said.

"Why would anybody want to hate the only father he'll ever have?" she asked. She looked down into the strainer as though it were a well of sorrow.

"Is that a serious question?" I asked. Because while I realized that Mom honestly believed in The Sanctity of the American Family, the lady also had an agenda, and she didn't brook subversives. One Bad Apple, and so forth. I think she worried I might contaminate her precious Michael. (It's a shame she didn't ask me about it, because I could have told her that when it came to the subject of The Catholic League, which was one of Michael's least favorite ways I had of referring to his family, he was as big a zealot as she was. In fact, Michael had a maddening way of spoiling romantic moments—like the long, coasting nights after he'd pick me up from the Playhouse, when, just as he seemed to have me dipped and buttered and rolled in bread crumbs, parked in the backseat of Dad's Lincoln, he'd say some perfectly exasperating thing, like someday we'd adopt children, and did I really have the heart to deny them a grandfather? Or was I really the kind of person to refuse his dear mother the chance to wheedle away Nana's powdered biscuit recipe?) "Mom," I said, "my father abandoned me for a jockey who doesn't ride sidesaddle, if you know what I mean."

But Mom didn't know what I meant. "You'll never have a good enough reason to love somebody," she said. "You either choose to love a person or you don't. Like your mother, for instance. You love your mother and there's nothing she could do to make you stop loving her, right?"

Since it's always seemed to me that the only great thing about heartbreak is that it gives you a funny story to tell later on, I hadn't exactly been shy about telling The One About My Mother. About The Time She Lied About Her Vagina Hemorrhaging, or whatever else I believed might make me sound whimsical or wise. So Mom wasn't the first person to point out my double standard when it came to loving my parents—that no matter what she did (and at the moment I was none too thrilled with her, since we practically hadn't seen each other since she met Peter), Mother and I were always basically fine. We shared an unstated pact granting the other the benefit of the doubt. But Daddy, he had to earn it. And because, for me, love was purely a matter of emotion, it seemed logical it would also be inconsistent. I didn't feel any obligation to love a man simply because we were relatives, and I told Mom so. "Well, Mom," I said, "I suppose *I'm* just not a person who can pick and choose whom I love."

I mean, really. *Whom*, no less.

What a twitty, ungrateful thing to say. Particularly since Yvella Leleux had chosen to love me ever since Michael first escorted me into her family room. What a horrible system of nature it is that a woman spends decades raising perfectly nice children who will eventually bring people home to defy her. But again, by the time Michael brought me home, Mom had seen it all, and was fairly unflappable. "You're probably just hungry, dear," she said. Which is what she always said when I was upset.

"I'm *not* hungry," I said. "Estrangement is my family tradition."

"I see," said Mom.

"On my mother's side," I continued.

"Hmmm," Mom said. She'd made a tidy stack of little curly bean tails on a folded paper towel.

"What?" I asked.

"Nothing," said Mom. "I was just thinking about how I need to get to know your mother better."

But I could see what was on Mom's mind. She was eyeing my mother like she was the Soviets and Mother was Yugoslavia. Well, best of luck to you, I thought. Where others have tried and failed. Just ask JoAnn and Nana.

"Run along, dear," said Mom, rising from the table, beans in hand. "I'm about to start cooking."

CHAPTER THIRTEEN

The Russians Are Coming

Michael played the fake violin when I predicted—while sitting in the shiny leather chairs of the airport terminal, as the January sun washed through the blue windows, and bounced off the white floors, and gave the day that strange, bright, and shadowy look of a memory—that Mother would never return to Texas. "Try to purge the drama from your life, JoAnn," Michael said to me. Because I'd made the mistake of telling him that's what my great-grandmother Eugenia said to my grandmother the day she left home, and Michael was the kind of person who enjoyed using family anecdotes against you.

"I'm dramatic," I told him. "But trust me, she's gone."

"You don't know that," he said. "What would make you say something like that?"

"Just a hunch," I said.

It was just a hunch, and the fact that Mother, in a black dress with red flowers like blood clots, looked over her shoulder three times as she walked toward the gate. And when the stewardess paged her seating category, it was the way her complexion mottled, like she'd eaten a bad oyster. And the way she'd hugged me so tight that a few strands of her plastic hair found their way into my mouth and tasted like a Nerf ball. It was all these things—but mostly, it was just a hunch.

"But she didn't even take an extra pair of shoes," Michael said. "She didn't even pack a suitcase. The woman's got a house full of furniture, Robert, and she's only known this Peter guy a couple of months."

"She doesn't care about any of that," I told him. "And I'm not saying she'll never come back. What I mean is that even if she doesn't marry Peter, she'll never really live in Texas again. She hates her life here."

"She looked fine this morning."

"It's the airport," I said. "She's always loved an airport."

"Well, that just doesn't sound like a mother to me," said Michael. "Leaving like that with nothing but an overnight case."

"You mean it doesn't sound like your mother," I said. (Michael's mother had recently told me she'd never, in her entire life, pumped gas into a car, which meant she'd never, in her entire life, driven farther than a tank of gas away from home.)

"I think maybe you're just hungry, dear," said Michael.

"Now that sounds like *your* mother," I said.

———

Yvella Leleux's personality may have packed the thrill of cheese, but I had to admit that there was warm reassurance in the fact that every time you went back to Mom, she was the same person. (Even her hair was always the same—I think my mother-in-law must have invented the flip in Gueydan, Louisiana, in the 1930s. It's the one and only hairstyle of her lifetime, worn since she was eight years old, and it's lent her appearance an unfaltering steadiness that makes the experience of flipping through photo albums positively eerie.) Mothers like mine may read better than mothers like Michael's, but mothers like his probably play better—"My mother can turn any day into a celebration," I once told him, "and your mother can turn a celebration into any day." But I found that moderation and consistency held their charms, as did the communal quality of the Leleux family, which was bustling and unfussy and boasted the added pleasure of being endlessly infantilized by Mom—who indulged our faintest whims until no one quite remembered how the Mr. Coffee worked without her.

While Mother was still in Texas, anxious to shake off any part of her life that slowed her procession to the altar, she saw Michael and his brood as a safe-exit strategy, a way of temporarily leaving me without leaving me alone. But as soon as she hit California, it was Mother who was alone—except, of course, for Peter, who had the depth of a mud puddle and the soul of a shoe. And that's when Mom put her plan to adopt my mother into action. There's a phrase in the horse business—nanny-goating—which refers to the fact that a stallion left alone in a stall will, from sheer wildness, rear and kick his way into the kind of broken-legged worthlessness that leads straight to the glue factory. But, if a nanny goat is allowed to live alongside the stallion, the horse, rather than trampling the goat, is soothed and civilized; he is "nanny-goated" by its company. In her coddling baritone (with the texture of banana pudding and the very essence of Valium) Yvella Leleux nanny-goated my mother long-distance. Because even though Mother made a couple of trips to Houston to collect her clothes, and have her hair reglued, and meet with her divorce lawyer, I'd been correct in believing that she was never really coming back from California.

After Mother had gone, I began to realize for the first time the enormity of the role she played in my life. And the reason I only got an inkling of the full figure of Mother's personality *after* she'd gone was because, as it turned out, there was really very little difference between Mother's impact locally and her impact coast-to-coast. There had been a part of me fairly fervent to be rid of both my parents and make some traction in adulthood alone with Michael. Of course, buried in the folds of the "alone with Michael" part was the take-one-step-forward-and-two-steps-back irony of Chester and Yvella, but they, I rationalized, could always be dealt with later. However, for a couple of reasons, rationalization was no match for Mother.

The first reason was that I'd internalized Mother so completely that I heard her voice at every turn—her manner of speech, her jokes, and even her little death songs.

The second reason was that I really *did* hear her voice at every turn, because the woman wouldn't stop telephoning. She started tracking Michael and me through our days like a great white hunter, resuming the kind of hands-on parenting she'd resigned from after Daddy left. She'd begin her afternoon rounds by ringing the Leleuxs; but failing to find us there, she'd have me paged—at the dollar movie theater where Michael and I often caught matinees, or at the nearby discount stores, or on the tatty sofa at Half Price Books, where we almost always wound up the evenings, drinking free coffee and reading whole books we had no intention of buying.

All I ever needed to hear to sell me on astrology was that Mother and Judy Garland shared June 10 for a birthday. So it didn't entirely surprise me that she acclimated to the booziness of Peter's lifestyle—which was just this side of alcoholic and not entirely of the modern era—as swiftly as she did. Mother had always been a problem drinker, but I'd never known her to get truly lit until she moved to California, when she started phoning for comfort, and crowing with stories about her rather luxurious fights with Peter, sounding like she'd just played the Palace. At a certain point, she even stopped saying good-bye, signing off her conversations instead by sort of crooning into the receiver, *"Good night, you beautiful people. Good night!"*

Most of Mother and Peter's Rather Luxurious Fights seemed to involve vodka and a boat, and also what she referred to as their bad luck with yacht clubs. Meaning they'd been muscled out of three of them by a series of piqued commodores for raising hell and ruckuses; for things like brandishing broken Smirnoff bottles, or shoving each other off barstools, or laying waste to the clubhouses they'd rented out for cocktail parties. Gradually, they developed a certain reputation among the local boating community that boded ill for their future, since, as Mother liked to say, "There are only so many places to park a yacht."

All of this I'd have found much more troubling if, in the retelling, Mother hadn't sounded quite so giddy with the glamour of her new life. Even on that murky afternoon she had me paged to the customer service booth of the army-navy surplus store to tell me she'd single-handedly grounded her flight home from Paris, causing Peter and herself to be booted from the plane in the midst of the Midwest for brawling in first class—for pouring a drink down his pants, then starting a striptease—Mother was unabashed and almost girlish. "After all, darling," she trilled from Indianapolis, "it's not as though I wasn't wearing a brassiere. And even still, it's all Peter could do to keep the airline from pressing charges."

And while I have to admit I wasn't completely immune to the unhinged allure of Mother's goings-on—because there's a part of me that's a real sucker for dark glamour, even when it's excruciating—a little of this goes a long way, believe me. I finally drew a hard line, refusing to answer the phone past three A.M. after a night when Mother called, frantic, from a pay phone on a pier to which she'd barely escaped in a dinghy after Peter threw her Goyard hatbox overboard, and then sailed into the black waters without her.

"Oh, Robert," she moaned. "I was forced to paddle for my very life."

"Isn't this a scene from an Elizabeth Taylor–Richard Burton movie?" I asked, still bleary-eyed from having been wrenched out of REM sleep. "*The VIPs*, maybe?"

"Be nice to her," Michael mouthed, lying next to me. He frogged my arm, and I pulled the blanket over his head. It always amazed me the way Michael could snap awake to enabling from a dead slumber.

"Where are you calling from, Mother?" I asked.

"I'm in the Delta," she said.

"You're in Mississippi?" I asked.

"The *California* Delta, Robert. California has a Delta, too," she said. "How many Mississippi yacht clubs do you know?"

"Mother," I said. "It's the middle of the night."

"Precisely," she said. "It's the middle of the night, and your poor mother has been abandoned on the docks. All I have left in the world is a wet hat and a dinghy."

"So what do you want from me?" I asked.

"A tender ear. A little compassion," Mother said.

"I'm hanging up the telephone," I said, because my quality of mercy had, finally, been strained.

"Let me talk to her," said Michael. He started tugging on the phone cord.

"Yes, let me talk to Michael," Mother said. "Let me talk to the son who cares whether his mother lives or dies. The one who worries about me getting gang-banged while I sleep in what amounts to little more than a raft."

"I'm hanging up now," I said, trying to hold the receiver out of Michael's reach.

"Don't you dare," he said.

"Old man river . . ." Mother sang.

Then, after Michael bit my elbow, and wrestled the phone from my grip, I slept with a pillow over my head while he listened to Mother reminisce about the bow blouse until Peter finally coasted back into the Delta, sobbing for forgiveness.

This was the beginning of a long string of late-night talks between Mother and Michael, who seemed to love each other a little more every time I fell asleep, until finally even Michael found he lacked the stamina for Mother's nighttime phone calls, mainly because he needed rest to keep pace with her daytime phone calls. His college GPA began to drop off, and that's when Yvella—who (fortunately, for our purposes) suffered from a terrible insomnia that often kept her up nights watching soap opera reruns—suggested that Mother begin calling her. In no time at all, Mother edged out *All My Children* as Yvella Leleux became Mother's tender ear, and more unexpectedly, her advocate.

"Your mother," Mom told me one morning over breakfast, in an admiring tone usually reserved for discussions of Erica Kane. "Your mother is a long-suffering woman."

"Isn't she just," I said, because even though I knew Mother believed she'd moved to California for our mutual benefit, and I *was* living off the pin money she managed to pilfer from Peter each month, I couldn't help being a tad bitter about the foreignness of her new life. Just as there was a part of me that had longed for independent adulthood, there was also a tiny piece, of which I was utterly ashamed, that missed my mommy. And for reasons I could barely understand, missing Mother made it almost impossible to talk to her in those first months of 1997. For a while, our phone conversations ended fast—after I said something hateful, and she asked to speak to Yvella, and I didn't blame her one bit. If it was comfort Mother wanted, she'd found the noted expert. Mom was accomplished in all The Gentle Arts of Womanhood, but her real specialty lay in rocking children to sleep.

And though I knew this, I still couldn't help being shocked that Mother was dopey enough to be lulled by Yvella's kind of comfort, which, from what I could overhear, seemed to consist of a big fat lot of Jesus Loves You, which, I'm sorry, is a bus that'll only take you so far, and then, it's that and a nickel, if you know what I mean. It made me think Mother must have needed family more than she'd ever let on, which made me regret every time I'd lost patience with her, and wonder whether (though *I'd* always been quite moved by the delicacy of my own feelings) I hadn't grown a little hard.

But honestly, spend a few hours with Michael and his mother and anyone would start to think his heart had turned to marble. Michael and Mom weren't just happy and sweet, they bought Christmas ornaments all year long. They watched competitive figure skating on television, and they couldn't begin to comprehend teasing. So after Mom succeeded in recruiting Mother into The Catholic League, she also sought to put a capper on my smart mouth. For instance, when I may have suggested, one evening after the stock report, that Mother was only one round of implants away from having her torso traded by OPEC, Mom rounded on me. "Do you think it's easy being a middle-aged woman?" she asked. "Suddenly alone, with only an oar to defend yourself? How would you like living away from your family, desperate to build a life for your son, without a place to park your yacht?"

"Just a little humor, Mom," I shrugged.

"Well, listen up, Ruth Buzzi," Mom said. (And I couldn't help noticing she was darning a sock.) "A joke's only funny if *two* people laugh."

"Depends on the two people," I muttered under my breath.

But I got the gist of Mom's point the first time Michael took me to a restaurant without laminated menus, and asked me what I thought of his sport coat, and I said something devastatingly Oscar Levant, and then Michael's bottom lip began quivering, and he started to cry. He'd never even heard of Oscar Levant. And at that moment, seeing him weep into his rather feral five o'clock shadow, I was struck—really blown a few paces back—by the realization that if I was going to form a life with Michael Leleux, I was going to have to become a nicer person. "Why would you say that to me?" Michael asked, gulping back a sniffle.

"I was only teasing," I said. "I love you."

"Well, that's not how you talk to somebody you love," said Michael.

Michael didn't find sparring or hysterics at all romantic.

There wasn't a tragic bone in his entire body. He found no pleasure in suffering. And though I loved Michael for his sweetness—he managed to be manly and tender at the same time, like a good rib-eye steak—it was sometimes a little provoking to be besotted with a man with a barrel chest and a wolfish slash of hair falling across his face like a scar, and whiskers the look of which made my stomach feel like fire whiskey, who absolutely refused to engage me in tortured romance. Because Michael didn't believe in tortured romance, because Michael believed that if two people didn't get married at the end of a movie, then it wasn't a romance.

"So *West Side Story* isn't, by your definition, a romance?" I asked Michael one evening when we'd gone parking in Dad's car, under the giant swaying pines of the state park—a place I loved going because it was practically free and didn't have telephone service, and Michael loved going because if I wouldn't let him stay at home he preferred the state park to driving aimlessly about the freeway system, which was my idea of a good time. (One of the many demoralizing things about coming from a stable home life is that it just decimates your sense of wanderlust. In general, Michael thought the fact that Mother and I spent so much time in airports signaled some kind of mental illness, even though I maintained that travel, in Texas, was too basic to be metaphorical, just like breathing wasn't metaphorical. It was just breathing.)

"*West Side Story* is, technically, a romance, it just isn't romantic," Michael said.

"Then what is it?" I asked.

"It's sad," he said.

"What about *Romeo and Juliet*?" I asked.

"Not romantic."

"And *Casablanca*?"

"Is this really how you want to spend the evening?" asked Michael. He scooted back to his side of the Lincoln's bench seat, and put both his hands on the steering wheel.

"I thought you were Catholic?" I asked. "What good is it falling in love with a Catholic if you don't get to savor torment?" Through the cracked window, I could hear the gentle slap of the lake against the nearby diving platform.

"I don't think denomination has much to do with wanting to be happy," said Michael.

"Aha," I said. "What about *The Thorn Birds*?"

"You know, Robert," said Michael. "I'd think you'd find it reassuring that the man who loves you doesn't happen to believe there's anything particularly deep about suffering."

"I do," I said. There were times, when Michael was frustrated, that his jaw seemed to throb in the most delicious way.

"Happy people can be just as deep as depressives, you know," said Michael.

"Is that why none of your mix tapes have ballads on them?" I asked. I moved a little closer towards Michael's side of the bench seat.

"I'd think you'd appreciate the fact that I believe in being happy," Michael said.

"And in happy endings?" I asked. I removed Michael's hand from the steering wheel.

"Consider the alternatives," he said.

CHAPTER FOURTEEN

A Bolt from the Blue

I'd long suspected Mrs. Rayburn—the geometry teacher at Trinity Lutheran who'd first convinced me to audition for *West Side Story*—of evil. She wore her hair in little-girl bangs, like Dorothy Parker, and told awful jokes about black people in outer space, and snickered every time the dumb girl, who couldn't determine the Probability of an Event to save her life, flossed her teeth with her hair. Sometimes Mrs. Rayburn would look at me, The Smart One, and roll her eyes like, Can you believe the mold spores we're forced to work with? And while this behavior did nothing to win me friends, it did provide those sweet jolts of superiority that persuaded me to postpone final judgment of Mrs. Rayburn.

All this changed, however, after Mildred, a walking party line from the Northwest Houston Community Playhouse, told Mrs. Rayburn I was living with Michael. Now, I know it's not entirely fair of me to blame Mildred—whose roots were as dark as her intentions and whose clothes were as loud as her gossip and whose every breath, when she wasn't panting details of the leather-sex affair she was carrying on with a ham actor who looked just like Charlton Heston, was spent blabbing about other people's love lives. Information loves freedom, and I was so contemptuous of anyone who might object to Michael and me, that at all places other than Trinity Lutheran High School, discretion was the last thing on my mind. I was seventeen and a half, and had been in love with a beautiful man for nearly six months! Michael was the point of ease and happiness in what then seemed a difficult life. It was maddening when people looked skeptically at me when I told them I'd love Michael forever—because I didn't yet understand that young love is the home of middle-age cynicism, and sex the home of anxiety, and that the common knowledge about romance is that it won't last. So I walked around telling people that, in order to have a great love story, a couple needed to be challenged. What would, say, Ronnie and Nancy be without their detractors? I asked. Boring, I answered. Well, blame it on my youth. And on having grown up the rich kid in a hick town, being the subject of gossip seemed trifling, and certainly nothing that might cause me harm.

But I no longer had the defenses (money or the protection of my parents) to stare down the natives. And though I didn't think of Michael as my secret, being in love with a man wasn't exactly something I wanted to discuss at my Evangelical Christian high school. There, I'd tried to keep all the changes in my life—my parents' divorce; our nouveau poverty; Michael and his family—private. Privacy wasn't an option, however, after Mrs. Rayburn invented for me an imaginary friend whom she began discussing, daily, in the course of my geometry class. An imaginary friend named Michael.

It began on a Friday in March, when the other students had been given an early start on their homework. Since the fall semester, I'd been working ahead of the rest of the class, and was waiting for Mrs. Rayburn to call me to her desk for my special assignment. I was antsy and bored. There were those rustling, late-afternoon sounds of pencils tapping plywood, and sneakers slowly dragging against chair legs. The spring sun, already warm, shone sweet and taunting through the windows. Finally, Mrs. Rayburn crooked her finger, and told me, "After you read through it, maybe you'd like to take the quiz at the end of Chapter Sixteen, and then bring in your answers on Monday?" So that it sounded like a question, but wasn't.

"Well, I won't like it," I joked. "But I'll do it." I leaned over Mrs. Rayburn's desk, writing page numbers in my datebook.

"I'd bet you'd like it if Michael told you to do it," Mrs. Rayburn said. Her eyes darted to catch my reaction, but her smile took a long time to spread across her face, like a drop of pigment slowly coloring a glass of water.

For a moment, it seemed possible I'd slipped into confusion, and was somehow failing to understand what was happening. *Had I really heard Mrs. Rayburn say Michael's name? Was there another Michael I'd forgotten?* I tried to check her inscrutable face—her cheeks were smoldering, but her bangs had fallen into a perfect triangle in the center of her forehead. So she looked wicked and cutesy at the same time. I said something that seemed safe, but was really pathetic: "What makes you say that?" I asked. Which must have given away everything she'd hoped for, because Mrs. Rayburn suddenly looked very satisfied—like she'd slowly built a snare, and had just heard its snap.

"Don't you have a special friend named Michael?" she asked. With that, the pigment bled through the water, and I knew precisely what was happening to me.

In March 1997, I was still young and stupid enough to think that hiding could protect me in some way that saying "Yes, I'm in love with Michael Leleux, and he and his family are the happiest part of my life" couldn't protect me. So I wasted the last opportunity I'd have to help myself, and gave Mrs. Rayburn all the permission she needed to blackmail and torment me for the rest of my time at Trinity. "I don't know what makes you say that," I said.

"Because I know I'm right," Mrs. Rayburn answered.

Then she turned to the rest of the class. "Hey guys," she said, very loudly, though I could barely hear her because my heart seemed to be beating in my ears. My classmates shot their heads up, grateful for any excuse to stop working. "Guys, would you like to know something very interesting about Robert?"

She cradled her chin in her hands and grinned. "Robert has a special friend named Michael." The tip of her tongue dashed across her teeth. "Michael's an imaginary friend, and Robert will do anything he wants. Isn't that right?" she asked me.

The class was confused. Mrs. Rayburn sounded like she was joking, so the less confident kids laughed. But most of them just made puppy expressions, certain they'd heard something rumbling about the house, but unsure as to what it had been. I tried to steer their reaction by laughing loudest, and by making goofy expressions to show I was, indeed, a fool. "Well, you know," I said, "I wouldn't do *anything* . . ."

"Oh, I think you would," said Mrs. Rayburn, happy to see me wriggling. "I think you'd do whatever Michael wanted." The students were still confused, but had comfortably settled into laughter.

"Nawww," I swatted my hand in the air. "I'm sure I'd draw the line somewhere." By now everyone had agreed it was a strange joke, but hilarious.

"Where?" asked Mrs. Rayburn. "Where would you draw the line?" It was the thrill of not quite knowing what we were talking about that fueled the laughter of the class. I put my finger to my cheek. I made my eyebrows into question marks and shrugged my shoulders. "I really don't know," I confessed. The class roared, and Mrs. Rayburn patted my arm. "I don't know where I'd draw the line," I said.

If only I'd paid closer attention in Coach Hambrick's theology class, I would have known that you can't strike a deal with the devil and hope to win. Because after freely parting with my dignity, after helping to establish Michael, my imaginary friend, as a joke, Mrs. Rayburn then turned him into a running gag. "Robert, what did you and Michael do this weekend?" she asked, soon after the bell rang Monday afternoon.

"Nothing much," I said. It was difficult to lift my eyes from my notebook, and play to the giggling of my class-mates.

"Oh, I bet you two did more than *nothing* together," she said.

Over the next several weeks, every time the lights flick-ered, Mrs. Rayburn made a ghostly whistle and blamed Michael. If the air-conditioning stalled, it was Michael's fault. After tut-tutting over the attendance sheet, she'd ask, "And Michael? Is Michael present today?" And the class shouted yes.

Then he began appearing in other classes. In the hallways, at my locker, people started asking: How's Michael doing? Is Michael here with you? Hi, Michael!

I laughed every time.

It was a brilliantly postmodern way to torture a young person. It proved Mrs. Rayburn to be tragically wasted in her job—there was a Beckett within her longing to be set free.

I never said a word about this to the real Michael, or to Mother. I was humiliated, and afraid they might confront Mrs. Rayburn, which at the time seemed like it would be even more humiliating. Since it was practically April any-way, I decided I could wait the school year out. No matter what happened, I figured, I'd be free of Mrs. Rayburn in a couple of months, and since Daddy's tuition checks had become erratic—sometimes bouncing, sometimes arriving late or not at all—I probably wouldn't even be welcomed back to Trinity for senior year, even if I was stupid enough to want to return, which I wasn't. Mrs. Rayburn, possessing a genius for these things, must have guessed this—both that I'd try to slither through the rest of the year, and not return for the next. So not wanting to waste a chance to do as much damage as possible, she waited a few weeks, then broached the subject of Michael—the real Michael, not the imaginary one—at a school faculty meeting.

I didn't notice until later, when the situation had burst open like a watermelon, but from that point on, the subject of gay people began popping into my classes. This should have been a difficult trend for me to miss. But my teachers had never served as figures of respect, and I'd always rather enjoyed their prairie prejudice. (Coach Hambrick said Julie Andrews embodied the nature of Satan: an angel who'd fallen from the heights of *The Sound of Music* into pervert flicks like *Victor/Victoria*.) Except for being terrorized in Mrs. Rayburn's class, I tended to drift through my days in a little fog of noblesse oblige. And in that fog, I tended to talk about love. A lot. Which is something oblivious young people are apt to do when they're as much in love as I was with Michael. In English class, we read *Wuthering Heights*, and when Catherine said she was Heathcliff, I said I was Catherine. For Coach Hambrick, I wrote a truly devastating essay about Ruth, and following your mother-in-law and her people being your people. During stolen moments, I read Lauren Bacall's *By Myself*, and talked to anyone who'd listen about Humphrey Bogart and knowing how to whistle. And Hellman and Hammett, blah blah blah. That spring, all the best clichés seemed fresh and glinty, and if I noticed the odd looks my teachers made in response to my enthusiasm at the very mention of The

Eternal Union of Souls, then I must have thought they were rolling their eyes at my coltishness.

They weren't, though.

Because, by that time, Mrs. Rayburn had told the faculty about Michael, and then someone told the headmaster, who knew the O'Dooles, who put him in touch with Daddy, who called his lawyer, who called Mother's lawyer, who called Mother in California, who paged me, one evening, at the dollar movie theater, where Michael and I sat watching *The Mirror Has Two Faces*.

"Thanks, Frank," I mouthed to Frank, the popcorn attendant, as he handed me the telephone over the refreshments counter. "Mother," I said. "I told you not to call me when I'm at the movies anymore. Poor Frank has to leave his popcorn machine, and it's so embarrassing to be called out of a dark theater, and somehow you always end up making me miss the best part."

"Don't worry," said Mother. "Peter and I saw that movie. There is no best part. Besides, this is serious. My lawyer called me today, in order to tell me that your father, and apparently everyone else in the state of Texas, is all up in arms because they found out you're living with, as they put it, 'some old homosexual man.' And my lawyer says you're going to have to stop staying at the Leleuxs'. At least as long as you're in that awful school, with the Christian Coalition reporting on your every move. Because how would it look in divorce court if That Bastard You Have For a Father says I'm paying for my seventeen-year-old son to live with his lover, Some Old Homosexual Man."

"Michael's only twenty-five," I said.

"You're not grasping the fine points here, darling," said Mother.

"Fine," I said. "Then I'm finished with school."

Mother whimpered.

"If my choice is living with Michael, or staying in school, then I'm living with Michael," I said.

"Why do you try to upset me?" asked Mother. "When I'm working so hard to improve your life? Why do you think I moved to California? Why do you think I'm living with Peter, if not to give *you* a better life?"

"Bullshit," I said to Mother. "Pardon my French, Frank," I said to Frank, who went to great lengths to promote a family atmosphere at the dollar theater. I lowered my voice: "My college tuition is *not* the reason you shacked up with Peter, Mother. Besides, you have Peter and Peter's yacht, and Daddy has Pam and their little love child, and who am I supposed to have? Nobody? Well, forget it. Besides, I don't really give a shit about your divorce trial," I told her. "Forgive me, Frank," I said to Frank. "Mother," I said. "I am quitting school tomorrow."

"You are *not* dropping out of high school," Mother said. "You will graduate, and then you will move to Manhattan, where you will become this generation's Truman Capote, and then you will tell everybody how goddamned wonderful I am. Who are you trying to be this week, Robert? Yvella? Do you want Yvella's life? Do you want to quit school, and marry some man, and spend your life cooking meals with canned pineapple rings and maraschino cherries for ingredients? Is that what you want?" Mother and I had often spoken about what a shame and pity it was that

Mom, who was really a gourmet when it came to Cajun food, was practically catastrophic when it came to plain American cooking.

Well, of course I didn't want a miserable life like Mom's—cutting my own hair, and spending the day in a bathrobe. And there were plenty of marvelous people— William Faulkner and Carrie Fisher, to name two—who never graduated from high school. But since I was furious with Mother, and I wanted to punish her, I said, "Well maybe that's just what I want. Maybe I do want to play Ruth to Yvella's Naomi."

"Well, puke," said Mother. "I'm getting off the phone now. I'm hanging up the phone, and I'm puking, and I'm buying a revolver, and I'm blowing my brains out, because I have an ungrateful child, and all you make me want to do is puke and die. Good-bye, Robert," said Mother.

"Good-bye, Mother," I said.

"I love you," she said.

"I love you, too," I told her. "One small Coke and one small Diet Coke, please," I said to Frank, handing the telephone over the counter.

I went back into the theater, and I gave Michael his Diet Coke. "How's your Mother?" Michael whispered.

"I'm quitting high school tomorrow," I said to Michael.

"You are not quitting high school tomorrow," he said.

"High school's not for everybody," I told him. "Just ask Mom." It drove Michael crazy that every time I complained about my homework, Mom said to me, "High school's not for everybody."

"Right," said Michael. "But Mom says Ronald Reagan caught Alzheimer's from thinking too hard."

"Hey," I said. "That's my joke."

"You are not quitting high school tomorrow," Michael said. "What did your mother say to you, anyway?"

"After the movie," I said.

"Out with it," Michael said, in the parking lot after the movie. "What did your mother have to say?"

"She said there was no best part to that lousy movie, and boy was she right."

"It must be something really horrible," Michael said. "You know how I know when something really awful has happened to you? When you're laughing. It's always when you crack dumb jokes that I know to grab a chair."

"She said her lawyer said I can't live with you as long as I'm enrolled in my high school. Because Mrs. Rayburn found out about us, and she told my whole school, and now my father knows, and his lawyer called and yelled at Mother's lawyer about my living with 'some old homosexual man.' "

"I can't believe it," Michael said. "Do I really look that old to you?"

CHAPTER FIFTEEN

Safe as Houses

It was shocking to learn, at *The Mirror Has Two Faces*, that Michael and I had become the focus of faculty conferences and the billable hours of my parents' attorneys. But it was no shock to discover that by the time we returned from the dollar theater, and Michael parked the Jaguar in his driveway on Pebble Springs Drive, my mother had phoned his mother, and the ladies had formed a plan. Stepping out of the car, I stretched my legs and breathed deeply, trying to repress the idea that the Leleuxs' house smelled like home. It was an idea I had to repress frequently, since I wasn't comfortable thinking of myself as that cozy kind of person who associates home with the smells of home cooking. But Michael's parents' house reeked with all those fortified, forever, old-people smells. It wasn't just the food: The ligustrum bushes blossomed sweetly by the garage, and the exhaust pipe from the clothes dryer gushed hot air through a grate in the side of the house, so the driveway was perfumed with the aroma of laundry detergent. And schmaltz or no schmaltz, it's a struggle not to be comforted by a house that smells like a warm towel—especially when your life is a miasma, as mine was that night.

Before Michael could even unlock the back door, we heard Mom's voice. She was sitting on the porch, drinking a cup of coffee under the electric bug-zapper, which occasionally punctuated her words with flashes of blue light. Mom's marriage had generally been a happy one, largely thanks to her belief that married people should avoid speaking to each other. Normally, Mom tried her best to keep Dad from interfering in the household arrangements. However, after Mother told Mom that Mrs. Rayburn described Michael as Some Old Homosexual Man, Mom and Dad didn't just talk, they argued. They yelled at each other in Cajun French over the solution to my troubles, and Mom won the day. Then she awaited our return from the movies on a reclining patio chair, in order to tell us everything, so that Dad wouldn't be tempted to pipe into the conversation. "Jessica and I have spoken," said Mom. "And don't worry. Because everything's handled."

"You bet everything's handled," I said. "First thing tomorrow morning, I'm dropping out of high school."

"You are not dropping out of high school," said Michael.

"You can just forget it, Mister," said Mom.

"Whatever happened to Education's Not For Everybody?"

"It's not for everybody. But it is for you," she said. "You *have* to go to college. Because if you didn't, you're the kind of person who would just end up bothering people, and making everybody miserable."

"Thanks," I said.

"I don't mean that ugly," said Mom. "You've just got a lot of nervous brain energy. You're like one of those hyper babies you've got to let run around the yard until they drop. Except in your case, it's thinking that's the trouble. I know. It's something I've prayed over."

"Haven't you ever stopped to realize . . ." I said to Mom. I reared my shoulders back, because I figured this was the sort of statement that might look really attractive with reared shoulders. "Haven't you even considered," I asked, "that nobody's listening to *your* prayers?"

"Watch it, Robert," said Michael.

"Now, now," Mom said to him. "That's a perfect example of what I'm talking about. If Robert doesn't go to college, it's gonna be that kind of thing all the time—mean, smart talk. And to tell the truth, I just don't have the energy for it. Not at my age. But it's okay," Mom said to me, "because after I talked to your mother, I called Little Sister."

"Oh, brother," I said. Little Sister was one of Michael's Louisiana cousins. She weighed three hundred pounds if she weighed an ounce, and if you closed one eye, she looked just like Sydney Greenstreet. Ever since Little Sister retired from the school cafeteria, Mom had increasingly relied upon her counsel. And after she'd advised Mom on the baby squirrels that got stuck in the bedroom wall, even I had to admit Little Sister's wisdom. "And what did Little Sister think?" I asked.

"Little Sister, your mother, Dad, and me—we've all agreed. For the time being, and for everybody concerned, the very best possible thing is for you to move into this house," said Mom.

"Dad said he thinks Robert moving into this house is the very best possible thing?" asked Michael.

"In his own special way," said Mom. Which meant that Dad had, at first, yelled, "Is this the reason I survived triple-bypass surgery?" but eventually relented. This was Dad's standard means of dominating his family—by telling us that every single day Jesus gave him since the bypass was a blessing, and we were all ruining it for him. "And," Mom continued, "Dad and I are gonna scoot some furniture around—maybe even call the Goodwill, and have some of it carted away—so you all can fit a bunch of Jessica's furniture in here from your old house. That way, when your Mother sells your house, you won't have to come up with so much money for storage." This was, I thought, an ideal solution, since it was one that Michael and I had already been secretly acting upon—sneaking my parents' furniture into his parents' house a lamp and a rug at a time. The fact that I'd been living on the verge of homelessness, while Michael lived in a big, barren house, had seemed so perfectly romantic—"like the son of the hotdog giant marrying the heiress of the mustard king," as Humphrey Bogart said in a movie one time.

"And you say Mother agreed to all this?" I asked. "I

don't understand. An hour and a half ago, she said I couldn't even spend the night here anymore."

"Your mother just fell in love with the idea as soon as we ruled out the alternatives."

"For instance?"

"Well, Little Sister pointed out that if your mother was so concerned with appearances, you could always go live with her and Peter in California."

"You suggested that to Mother?"

"Yes. And she said that, on the other hand, a person can't live life by the dictates of convention."

"That's very brave of her."

"Stop quibbling, Robert," said Michael.

"After all," said Mom, "as Sister pointed out, you'll be turning eighteen in September. And as long as you're not going to that mean old school anymore, and you've got your high school diploma, what possible difference could it make to anybody if you live here with our family?"

"But, how does Little Sister think I'm going to get a diploma if I drop out of Trinity?"

"On that point, Sister was at a loss. For this, we have Beano to thank."

Now don't get me wrong. I'm sure Mom's faith in the ability of her family to solve any problem was very quaint in its own adorably ethnic way, sort of like Santeria. But it didn't take long for the system to run away with itself, at least as far as I was concerned, and then you were left with Louisiana cousins of ever more tenuous kinship—with people, in short, like Beano. (I admit I've only actually met Beano once, at a funeral, and have been given to understand

she's a very nice person—it's just that I find myself consti-
tutionally incapable of identifying with a Beano.)

"Well," Mom sighed. "We couldn't have made it without Beano, because she told me to call my sister Ruby, who
suggested I call my sister Mary, who insisted I call my sister Zelima, who has a daughter who's practically a Communist and makes paintings I can live without and little
political dolls that look just like voodoo to me."

"Kay," said Michael.

"Exactly," said Mom. "Well, Kay lives in a little hippie
town called Elk, up near Oregon, and has a friend who's a
real nice lesbian lady, with a part-time job filing records
for the school system." (There were moments when the
efforts of Michael's family reminded me of that part in
One Hundred and One Dalmatians when the dogs start a
bark that works its way across England.)

"So I called Kay, and she was just pleased as punch to
hear from me, because years ago I helped Zelima sew her a
fancy dress during rush week at LSU. And I told her about
Robert's school, and his parents' lawyers, and Michael being slandered as Some Old Homosexual Man, and, in general, how Robert was just being bound and flayed like a
Christian martyr. Then Kay said she thought he was being
persecuted like a political dissident. Then we both agreed
that what he really needed was asylum."

"And Kay of Elk will grant me asylum?" I asked.

"Well, she started asking me a slew of questions about
all the classes you've taken," said Mom. "And I told her
about you and all those advanced placement courses, and
how you've got real good grades, and how, at this rate, you

might even make valedictorian. So Kay got real excited, because she's pretty sure the graduation requirements up there are real different than they are in Texas. So she wants to take a peek at your paperwork. And who knows, if she can get you qualified for residence, it's possible you could hop right up to Elk for six months or so, and graduate there. And by that time, you'll have turned eighteen, and everything around here will have cooled down, and you can come back and live with us happy ever after."

"You accomplished all of this in the last hour and a half?" I asked. This was particularly shocking in light of the fact that Mom was one of the planet's slowest humans, capable of making the most meager task last hours. It took about three days for Mom to repot an azalea bush, and don't get me started on the way the woman tenderized a chicken, which was something straight out of *Zen and the Art of Archery*.

"Desperate times and desperate measures," said Mom.

"So I could just dash up to Zelima's daughter's school for a few months, and then be done with it?" I asked.

"Well. Kay won't be sure until she sees your paperwork . . . ," said Mom. "But Michael could visit all the time."

"This sounds very unbelievable. And fishy," I said.

"Don't look a gift fish in the mouth," said Michael, who was much too sweet for wit. I shook my head at him, and patted the dear thing on the shoulder.

"And this woman, Kay, Zelima's Communist daughter, she doesn't know me from Adam, and just because you made her some sorority dress fifteen years ago, she'd be willing to do me this big favor?"

"Kay said it was an issue of Each According to His Ability," said Mom. "Besides, it was a real pretty dress. And she ended up pledging that sorority."

"Be that as it may," I said. "This is never going to work."

"How do you know?" asked Michael.

"Because if this were a television show, then this would be a *zany* television show," I said.

"You exaggerate everything," said Michael.

"Can you predict the future?" Mom asked me.

"No," I admitted, since it had been recently established that I couldn't. "But, if it *does* work, then I'm converting to Catholicism—as soon as they, you know, get on the bus with the whole gay thing. And maybe Communism, too. What the hell, I'll be a Catholic Communist."

"Let's not get carried away," said Mom.

"I have nothing to lose," I said.

"Kay swears it'll be just as easy as pie."

"Famous last words," I said.

But this time, and for two reasons—the first being that as long as I got to quit Trinity, I couldn't have cared less about Mom's plan; and the second being that relying upon the largesse of Zelima's hippie daughter, Kay of Elk, for my high school diploma, was so all-around stupid, and stank, from its conception, of catastrophe—the whole scheme went off without a hitch; even better, in fact, than anyone could have anticipated. It was just one more example of life's nonlinear magic; one more instance of God behaving like an alcoholic parent, one moment betraying your trust by denying the simple, easy requests like exact change and convenient parking spaces, the next yanking your faith back like a yo-yo by granting the most outrageous, faintly made wishes. The following morning, Mother made phone calls and sent faxes to Trinity Lutheran and Zelima's hippie daughter; Mom and Dad secretly sent money to Kay, to help cover the cost of keeping me; and I, humbling myself, called JoAnn, who paid for my plane ticket and bus fare to Elk, a utopian perch on the cliffs of the Pacific.

Each of the four days I spent in Elk was like living on the other side of the mirror. Kay had spread word of my story—and because Mrs. Rayburn had tortured me for being gay, the villagers of Elk greased my path. Complete strangers went to lengths on my behalf, and none more than Mr. Pepper, a high school counselor in harem pants whose profession was encouragement, and whose intention it was to make me believe I could accomplish anything through education. So, on my first day in Elk, it was my challenge to make Mr. Pepper believe that all I wanted to accomplish was a diploma. "But Kay tells me you've got quite a talent for drama!" said Mr. Pepper, as we conferred in his office, plastered with posters of people, like Gandhi, as well-intentioned and humorless as himself.

"I have no talent for drama," I explained. "What Kay probably meant was that I'm dramatic. Sometimes people get them confused. Can you tell me what I need to graduate, Mr. Pepper?"

"And then there's writing! We have a wonderful gay man who teaches creative writing!"

"I'm sure he's a peach, Mr. Pepper. But is creative writing a class I need in order to graduate?"

"Well, no," he confessed, his exclamation points withering.

"Then what do I need?"

Mr. Pepper retrenched, and opened a manila folder on his desk. "Civics," he sighed.

"Just civics?"

"Just civics," he said. "It's the strangest thing. You seem to have taken a perfectly staggering number of theology classes. All of which I've considered electives. Then, there's the AP courses. So, from the perspective of credit hours, you've actually taken several more classes than you need to graduate. Except for civics. All you lack to graduate is one measly civics class."

"And is there a work-at-home option?" I asked, because I'd noticed Zoe, Kay's daughter, taking a class on her home computer.

"Oh, sure," said Mr. Pepper. Slamming my manila folder shut, he closed the book on me. "I mean, why not?"

"Mr. Pepper," I said. "You're a prince."

I lugged my civics book back to Kay's house, worked through my first and second nights in Elk, and on the third day returned to Mr. Pepper, having completed the coursework. "You mean you're ready for your next assignment already?!"

"Nope," I said. "I mean I'm finished with the entire class. I mean I'm ready for my final exam." I could have sworn I glimpsed a tear in poor Mr. Pepper's eye. And he looked positively bittersweet while marking an A on my final, and later, when I asked him to mail my scarlet, leather-bound diploma to 4315 Pebble Springs Drive, and could he possibly give me directions to the bus stop?

So, on my third evening in Elk, I packed my bags. And on the fourth, though it was contrary to The Plan, and I wasn't eighteen, and Dad clutched his heart and groused in Cajun French, I took the first plane back to Houston, and Michael. Who, upon my arrival, began, with his mother, sending away for local college catalogues—for fear I'd drive the house crazy.

CHAPTER SIXTEEN

The Fire Next Time

The most wonderful part of befriending a country-western singer is that they don't mind listening to you whine—whining being, after all, their bread and butter. Aside from being Michael's best friend, Jessica Phillips was a country-western singer with a voice like a hot, glazed doughnut and a bosom as big as her heart and her hair. She loved to sing so much she'd book any gig in Texas. So Michael and I often spent Saturday mornings in Jessica's truck, driving halfway to Louisiana, her pet boxers rolling like tumbleweeds through the backseat, just so Jessica could sing "Blue Moon of Kentucky, Won't You Keep on Shining" in a honky-tonk, or a used-car lot, or even a Jehovah's Witness fashion show at a Chinese food restaurant. Jessica was one of those Southern women who live in a constant state of moral outrage over things like *60 Minutes* letting its male newscasters wear earrings. And since Jessica was Michael's best friend, and since complaining was my new favorite thing, Jessica and I quickly became best friends, too. She always had something fresh and furious to say, which was fortunate for our friendship, because throughout the spring of 1997, I only had two things to say—my parents had abandoned me, and my life was a tragedy.

As soon as something particularly heinous happened to me, I could hardly wait to find a phone and call Jessica. Say, when Mother told me Peter was buying a Porsche. "And it's a *convertible*," I told her. "Talk about staying too long at the fair."

To which Jessica replied, "I just hate the name Misty. I mean whose big idea was it to start naming babies after forms of precipitation?"

But Jessica could just as easily have said, "I'm sure I'm not the first person to mention to you how much more a taco salad costs at McDonald's than at Jack in the Box." Or "Don't you just live in mortal terror of having a finger lopped off?" Or "Can somebody please explain to me why we have more Coca-Colas to choose from than presidential candidates?"

Jessica and I never seemed to be having the same conversation. But that didn't bother me, because I found her personality to be as contagious as the clap, and her cowgirl-toughness gave me confidence. Though I will confess another of the reasons I treasured her friendship was because it drove Mother absolutely up a wall and down the other side whenever I told her how truly heartbroken I was not to be able to spend the day chatting with her on the telephone, because The New Jessica was picking me up to go to a rodeo. "A *rodeo*, Robert?" Mother asked me.

"Jessica's singing 'San Antonio Rose,' " I said.

"I see." I heard the flame pop in her cigarette. "Tell me, Robert. What do you think a psychiatrist would make of the fact that the day I left town, you made best friends with another blonde from Texas whose name is also Jessica? Doesn't this friendship seem a little unusual to you?"

"No, Mother," I said. "You know how Jesus hates a vacuum."

So, of course, on the wispy May evening when Mother tracked me to the frayed sofa at Half Price Books—where Michael sat reading Martha Graham's *Blood Memory*, and I finished the last half of Barbara Goldsmith's *Little Gloria . . . Happy at Last*—to inform me that I was about to be flung, along with all my earthly possessions, out of our home like *The Grapes of Wrath*, my first instinct was to phone Jessica, certain the two of us could harmonize my predicament into song.

I was skimming a particularly juicy passage regarding the Marchioness of Milford Haven when Burl, the bookstore's rather husky evening manager—with whom Mother had managed, over the past several months, to strike a particular rapport—called me to the telephone. "Hello, Mother," I said into the receiver.

"Have you ever noticed," Mother asked me, "how much Burl sounds like Yvella over the telephone?"

"Only during pollen season," I said. "The rest of the year Mom's voice is much deeper."

"Darling," said Mother. "I have the most marvelous news. I hope you don't mind I told Burl first."

"Peter pickled his liver?" I asked.

"Even better," she said. "Your bastard grandfather finally agreed to buy me out of the house. And at my price, too. Of course, we won't get a nickel until the divorce papers are signed. But at least this whole ordeal is nearly over."

"Congratulations, Mother," I said.

"Don't congratulate me. This is our great news, Robert. I'll be able to send you more money. And we'll both be able to move on with our lives. . . ."

"That *is* marvelous news," I said. The print in *Little Gloria* . . . suddenly grew fuzzy, as my mind clouded with thoughts of Michael's remaining college credits, and the cost of Manhattan studio apartments.

"And speaking of moving on," Mother said. "I'm going to need your help."

My mind swirled like a candy cane with little needlepoint thoughts about Jesus closing a door and opening windows. "Sure," I said.

"Well," said Mother. "It's like I told you. You and I, we're not going to get a dime of that money until the divorce is finalized. But in the meantime, I told my lawyer to tell your father's lawyer that we'll be out of that house as soon as possible. By the end of the month, even. But the thing is, darling, Peter's going to Tokyo on business, and it's absolutely vital that I go with him."

Mother had a knack for making a vacation sound like a UNICEF tour. "So you're not coming back to help me?" I asked. All clouds suddenly lifted: My mind was very clear.

"Now, you know it's in both our interests that I marry Peter pronto, and I don't know how you expect that to happen if we're in different hemispheres."

"But you are going to pay for a moving company, right?" I found myself leaning against Burl's desk for support.

"Robert," said Mother. "How many different ways do I have to tell you that we don't have one goddamned cent? Let's give this one another try: *We don't have one goddamned cent.*"

"Can't you ask Peter for the money?"

"And wouldn't that be romantic. Now, listen up. I've already talked to Yvella, and she's just certain Michael will help you. And his sisters, and their husbands, they might even pitch in, too. And she's absolutely guaranteed me a little corner of her attic for some of our old furniture, and maybe in the garage and a few rooms around the house, too, but on that, she'll have to get back with me."

"But you've got money for a storage unit, at least?"

"Try to concentrate, Robert. Because for some reason, you and I aren't communicating. I have *no* money. Right now. Nothing. In the past I *had* money, and in the future I'll *have* money, but *now* there's just nothing. *Comprenez-vous?*"

"Well, if they were running a special on collagen at the Safeway, you'd manage to come up with the money."

"I need you to be an adult." Mother sighed. "I need you to find a way to make things happen. And I also need to get off the telephone. Now, I love you very much, you beautiful person. Good night."

"Sayonara," I said, before Mother hung up.

"How's your mother?" Michael asked, without looking up from his book.

"She sold our house," I said. I sat down next to him. "And now she's going to Japan. And I have to move everything out of the house by the end of the month." Michael looked up, and saw that my face was dancing. This was an unsettling new development. Since the dodgy end of my high school career, I'd found that I'd stopped crying when I was upset. Instead, my hands shook, and my neck turkey wobbled, and my eyes got blinky. It made me look like Mount Saint Helens and it was not very attractive.

"Baby," said Michael.

"She's not coming back to help me," I said. "She said that you'd help me."

"Well, of course I'll help you," said Michael.

"Well, of course you'll help me, Michael," I said. "That's not the point."

"Oh, sweetheart," said Michael. He stroked the hair back from my face. "You're surprised by how much it'll hurt you to leave home, aren't you?"

"Are you daft?" I asked. I swatted his hand away. "I only wish I could torch the dump. No, the point is that I don't know how to do anything. I don't know how to pack up a house. Or move furniture. Or rent a truck, or anything."

"And that's why I'm the perfect man," said Michael. "I've moved to New York and back so many times I can do it in my sleep. I'll handle it," said Michael. "I'll talk to my family."

"Christ on crutches," I said. (This was my absolute favorite of a series of Vacation Bible School expletives employed by Michael's family.)

"We could always call *your* family," said Michael.

"Is that a dagger I see before me?"

"That's what I thought," said Michael. "We'll stick with mine. My sisters. Their husbands. Everybody's gonna help."

"That's what your mother told my mother," I said. "But why would they do that?"

"Because that's the system," said Michael. "If they don't help, the whole system falls apart."

"We'll see how the system holds up in this case," I said.

"Come on," said Michael. "Let's go home."

But we didn't go straight home. Because, first, I called Jessica, who warned me never to take a cruise to Belize on account of the human botfly, and then offered to treat us to Whataburgers. And while we sat eating in the parking lot, she offered her pickup, her help, and her husband for my move. And then she did something that absolutely betrayed the terms of our friendship, not to mention my sense of violation: She gave me good advice. "All I can tell you," I'd moaned through a thick bite of cheeseburger, "is that I just didn't see this coming."

"But, hon," she said. "Do you ever?"

I almost choked on an onion ring. "Do I ever what?" I asked.

"Do you ever see things coming? Predict the future, I mean. Maybe you've got some crystal ball you've been hiding?"

I felt like throwing my strawberry milkshake right in her face. "As a matter of fact," I said. "Yes. Under normal circumstances, I *can* be fairly certain of my future. I *can* predict what will happen to me. Given that I plan things out and schedule carefully."

Jessica chortled, and fed a french fry to Fallon Carring-ton, the boxer sniffing over the car seat. "Honey pie," she said to me, "life is not a layaway plan."

"Well, pardon me." This must be what passes for wis-dom at the Grand Ole Opry, I thought to myself. "But I'm afraid I don't know much about layaway plans."

"I didn't know much about them when I was your age, either," said Jessica. "But after my daddy died when I was eight years old—which, by the way, was the first thing I didn't see coming—Mama married a fat Greek man. And Constantino Papapapoulos was, by the way, the sec-ond thing I didn't see coming. He owned a big chain of dry-cleaners, and ate so much lamb and feta that his cardi-ologist told him to jog, in order to improve his circulation. So Constantino started running marathons, and lost a ton of weight, and started to get that puddle-skin look. Kind of like a shar-pei.

"Well, one morning at the starting line, Mama said, 'See you later, Constantino,' because she wanted to get a corny-dog from the concession stand. And by the time Mama ate it, and made it to the finish line, there lay Con-stantino. Dead dead dead. The paramedics dropped a sheet over his head, and said his fat little heart just popped like a firecracker. And of course, at the time, Mama and I thought this was the worst thing that could *ever* happen. But after the funeral we found out it wasn't. Because not only had Constantino driven the dry-cleaners into bankruptcy, so they weren't worth a plug nickel, but he also had another wife—a Greek who was shaped like a boot, with a mus-tache, and a face like Anna Magnani, and a whole passel of

Constantino's fat babies all rolled up like grape leaves. So then Mama had to start selling Japanese knife sets, and my brother had to work banquets at the Holiday Inn, and I started buying all my dresses on the layaway plan, because Mama wouldn't let me spend a penny of the money my daddy left me. And not any of that, Robert. Not one iota," Jessica said. "Did I ever see coming."

This was Jessica's way of comforting a person. By telling a story so ghastly you ended up grateful not to be selling Japanese knife sets. "Yep," I said. "That's a terrible story." A little grudgingly, because I thought Jessica could have at least waited until I finished my cheeseburger to trump my miserable story.

"No," said Jessica. "That's the price of tea in China."

"Well, that may be so," I said. "But I just have to hold out a little longer. The beauty of my situation is that, from here, things can only get better."

Fallon Carrington howled.

"Famous last words," Michael said.

"Didn't you hear a word I just said about Anna Magnani?" Jessica asked.

May is summertime in Texas. And three weeks later, on the Saturday morning The Catholic League descended upon my parents' house, plump white clouds lounged under the hot sun like American tourists on their first trip abroad, and wildflowers were sneaking, like small children awake in a sleeping house, through the sprouted grass, which was that thumping, newly living green. And though the task of packing away years of my parents' life had been horrifying and backbreaking, leaving me with the belief that *no one* had *ever* moved before, I had, through a mixture of sleeplessness and a growing excitement, scored the giddy sense of escaping a gloomy life, and I couldn't work fast enough. So by the time Michael's family arrived a bit before noon with a borrowed flatbed truck, Jessica, Michael, and I had boxed, wrapped, and taped almost everything I hadn't decided to leave behind for Daddy. And by midafternoon, Michael and I had, with his brothers-in-law, loaded the furniture onto the truck, and the boxes into their cars and Dad's Lincoln, and begun driving down the road.

Michael and I followed the truck in Dad's spare Impala, with the windows rolled down because it didn't have air-conditioning. Lamps wrapped in T-shirts and candlesticks wrapped in newspaper were piled on the seats beside us. And as we drove down the road, the breeze made our bodies, sticky with sweat, feel cool and wet, and long strands of our hair flapped into the air and our eyes. I slipped off my sandals, and folded my legs up on the dashboard, looking at the layers of sheer filth that caked the soles of my feet from working without my shoes. Michael kept fiddling with the knobs on the radio, surfing for music that would keep us awake. "You feeling okay about this?" Michael asked.

"I'm not feeling anything about this," I said. Which was the happy truth; I was too numb and exhausted even to fully appreciate the fact that if I chose to, I never had to return to Petunia, Texas. And even if I did come back, it would never again be as someone who lived there.

No matter which way Michael turned the dial, he met thick fields of static. So he turned the radio off, and said, "Well, you're out of that house. You're off the O'Dooles' ranch. That's what you said you've always wanted. And someday soon, we're going to have our own apartment, I promise." I laid my head against the seat and, closing my eyes, let my fingers run through the wind rushing outside the car.

And then I flinched as something stung the inside of my wrist. I sat up, fast, unfolding my legs and setting them on the floor saw there was something wet dripping down my arm from the spot where I'd felt the sting.

Then a fat drop of rain slapped against the windshield, just above the wide crack that ran across the glass.

Michael and I leaned forward in a single movement, and craned our necks over the dashboard, squinting into sunlight in search of a dark cloud. But there was none. Each was a cotton ball, or sugar lump, nestled harmless and cozy into the easy blue sky.

We leaned back, with our jaws cocked and listening: for something to strike the metal of the roof, for another slap on the glass . . .

Two more raindrops collided against the windshield.

And another against the shining chrome of the driver's-side mirror.

And suddenly, from the blameless bright blue day, it was raining. I climbed across the seats to roll up the windows, and Michael switched on the wipers.

And then it was pouring. So heavy that despite the wipers' pounding, the world seemed smeared in sunlight, and the flatbed truck, loaded with all of the furniture from all of the rooms I'd ever lived in, looked like a color-spot floating before the car.

I sat back against the seat, and rubbed my fists against my eyes, and twitched, and groaned, "Oh, my God." Which was appropriate, since there was something almost metaphysical about this wave of bad luck.

"It's about to stop," Michael said. "It's going to just stop. This is just one of those, you know, those springtime bursts of rain, and it won't have time to soak into the upholstery or anything."

There was a sudden thud, as a sheet of rain slammed itself, with the heft of a longhorn steer, against the hood of the car.

My eyes started blinking, fluttering like hummingbirds, and my neck began to quiver. We were caught on an open country road, with no shelter, and steep ditches. And on either side of us was empty pasture.

There was nothing to do but drive forward.

Anna Magnani, indeed.

CHAPTER SEVENTEEN

Half a Loaf

I 've yet to discover my métier." That was my favorite
dumb thing to say to Tina Marie, or The New Jessica,
or worst of all, my grandmother JoAnn, during the months
I spent waiting for the furniture to dry. It was a line I'd
culled from a paperback biography of Princess Lee Radziwill, and because it sounded better than "I watch TV," it
seemed like the perfect answer to the question, "Robert,
what the hell are you doing with your life?" I abandoned it,
however, after discovering "I'm afraid you'll find me rather
idle," which was something Catherine Deneuve said in a
vampire movie, and lasted longer—roughly the year it took
the sofa springs to quit making rusty, screen-door noises,
and for the velvet chairs to lose that peculiar crunching
quality they developed after their soaking.

My local college plans were snuffed in the fall of 1997, to
the chagrin of Michael and Mom, for lack of wherewithal.

Mother's progress in scoring my tuition money, by herding Peter into matrimony, was lagging. And my hopes of a scholarship ended in tears one afternoon, when I was dismissed from the office of Jefferson Davis, a financial aid counselor who looked at Michael and me like we were Fort Sumter, then grinned at us and said that without both my parents' tax returns, I didn't qualify for a penny of financial aid. And because I was young, and had yet to be enlightened by Hannah Arendt on the banal-evil that lives in the hearts of middle-income paper-pushers; and I wasn't about to track Daddy down for his tax returns, no matter what Michael might say; and when I asked Mother, she said, *"Taxes? I don't pay taxes,"* I decided, for the time being, to forget college, and dream another dream. So after Michael's cousin, Kay of Elk, engineered my high school graduation, I forayed into the labor force.

Briefly.

Because, despite my initial enthusiasm, my blue-collar days were destined to end in tragedy.

I didn't know how to *do* anything. The boy jobs were hopeless, because I couldn't operate machines, and my magnolia-fair skin fried like catfish in the Texas sunshine. And the girl jobs were goners, too, because I couldn't add, type, or alphabetize. What remained, then, was The Seventh Level of Hell: waiting tables and checking groceries. And since, when I finally wheedled an interview at a ribs restaurant, I told the manager, when he asked what I wanted to do with my life, that I'd yet to discover my métier, there was nothing left for me but to glaze hams at the Honey Ham Sandwich Shop, blowtorching meat-slabs on a Lazy Susan. For which I thanked my lucky stars, since I'd reached that state of hardscrabble unemployment when you really don't mind picking up the propane kegs on your way to work in the morning.

I surprised myself by developing a real fondness for glazing, because even I was capable of operating a blow-torch (though I twice set the wall afire), and it was possible to Zen-dissociate from the wretchedness of my circum-stances by staring deep into the licking blue flame. And, anyway, it was lollipops compared to the other half of my job—slicing the meat. Which was horrible, and terroriz-ing, because the electric meat-slicer was a big, antique, ricocheting contraption of torture and death that, daily, short-circuited and electrocuted me. And it's hard to over-state the trauma implicit in knowing, as you swing by the truck stop for that morning's propane supply, that you will be, at some creeping, unnumbered moment of the work-day, pumped with enough voltage to wire Cleveland.

Michael demanded I quit, and I could have, with Mom and Dad footing the bills, and Mother's mad money. But I had jumbled ideas of bravery-under-reduced-circumstances, and thought that if Lillian Hellman or Mame could work retail at Macy's, then I could absorb a few stray jolts. Also, after my string of crises, I decided that if I could only—through sheer application and no matter how painful—force success out of one small thing, like ham, then I could begin to turn my life around. I had to start somewhere, and I figured that place might as well be the Honey Ham Sandwich Shop.

Then one morning, while lacing my low-tops and con-templating the possible long-term neurological conse-quences of being regularly shocked so hard my fillings sizzled, I started heave-sobbing with animal terror and self-pity. Michael cradled me and said, "If you won't quit, then at least insist on a promotion."

So after righteously marching into the office of Gale, the owner of the Honey Ham Sandwich Shop, and declar-ing (with flashes of Cesar Chavez) that I was drawing the line, and just plain refused to be electrocuted anymore, I was promoted to the cash register. Which was the begin-ning of the end. Because, as it turned out, the cash register was significantly more complicated than the blowtorch. So complicated, in fact, that I never really understood its mysterious inner workings, but faked it for fear of being banished back to the meat-slicer. Specifically, I never learned how, after making an error in tallying a cus-tomer's order, to clear the sale and begin anew. Instead, I tended to continue wantonly adding sums, and then sub-tracting them, over and over, until I reached amounts that seemed suitable, but somehow gave the shop's accountant the impression that thousands of dollars' worth of ham sandwiches were being trafficked out of the store. At which point I was fired, along with my manager, a lank single mother who was habitually beaten by some man in her life and who harbored truly pathetic hopes of someday buying the shop and turning it into a *gourmet* ham sand-wich store.

It seemed positively fascist that a trounced and faded lady should suffer for my failings. So I tried to explain my mistakes to Gale. "You see, Gale," I said, "the cash register was a mistake for me. It was too much too soon. We know that now. But you have to admit I had finesse with the blowtorch. If you'd only move me back to the blowtorch, I know this whole situation would resolve itself." I even told her that, on the condition she provided me with insulated gloves of some kind, I'd be willing to return to the meat-slicer, if only she'd pardon my poor manager. But Gale was unmoved. And knowing that I hadn't just failed, but had also cost a desperate woman her job, was devastating, and crippled my confidence.

When I was growing up, Mother told me that in her day, Texas sororities lumped potential pledges into two cate-gories: "Some girls are flowers," Mother repeated, with a cruel, cold Darwinian shrug, "and others are pots." She'd given this to me like a coat, so I could smugly wrap myself in the comfort of being a flower at Beckendorf Junior High, while my classmates perforated me for being a fairy.

But Mother hadn't exactly proven herself the steadiest hand at the judging of character (she wanted to marry Pe-ter, for crying out loud). After more than proving myself a washout at the Honey Ham Sandwich Shop—after, in fact, wreaking havoc on the lives of the sweet, humble pots surrounding me—I began to worry I'd overestimated my-self all along. There was a bad smell hanging in the air, and I began to wonder whether it was coming from me. "Oh, Michael," I wailed, wiping my nose on a striped boating shirt I'd found at the junk store, and which was absolutely identical to the one I'd seen Jackie Kennedy wear while reading Witold Rybczynski at a picnic in *Star* magazine. "I feel like such a fool." My shoulders wobbled. "All this time, I thought I was a flower. But I can see it now. I'm a pot."

Michael squeezed me on one of the sofas that still smelled ever so slightly of mildew. He did his best to comfort me, but since he hadn't been schooled in the razing euphemisms of the Sisterhood, I didn't feel he quite grasped my desolation. "Baby," he said. He was slightly confused, but stringing along. "You're not a pot. You're a flower."

"Oh, face facts, Michael," I barked. "I'm a pot."

"Sweetie, no. A flower. You're one great big flower."

"Do you really mean that?" I sniffled. "You're not just being kind?"

"Of course not," he said. Michael retrieved a box of Kleenex from Mom's coffee table. That was one of the marvelous parts of suburban middle-class life—big, tacky cardboard boxes of Kleenex popped up everywhere.

"You really think I'm a flower?" I asked hopefully. I blew my nose, and looked imploringly into Michael's eyes.

"Absolutely."

"What kind?"

"Pardon?"

"What kind of flower would you say I am?"

"What kind . . . I . . . don't know," said Michael. He looked panic-stricken. He was desperately flipping through seed catalogues in his mind, terrified I'd start crying again.

But it was too late. I started bawling so hard I choked, and Michael looked thwarted.

"I need you to level with me, Michael," I said as soon as I could speak again. "If I can't even cut it glazing hams,

what hope do I have in the wider world? Let's be honest—
I'm at rock bottom. Besides you, my life is a debacle. What
could possibly be left for me after this?"

"Sweetheart, I think it's possible that a person could fail
as a ham-glazer, and still retain some hope of being a writer,
for instance. If I were you, I'd think of this experience as
material."

"Material I've got plenty of," I said. "I've reached my
quota on material."

Michael rubbed his temples. "I certainly hope not," he
said.

"Why?" I asked.

"Because then you'd have to stop living your life like a
story."

Well, Michael could make fun all he wanted, but in for-
lorn moments especially, it comforted me to take a narra-
tive approach to life. Because if I could match my experience
to the character in a book or movie, it seemed possible I
was heading towards some glorious future. And though it
might sound stagy to recycle old dialogue, I found it
helped to preserve my dignity—after, say, being shocked
by an electric meat-slicer—to place myself in the company
of a movie star or a princess, even a fake princess who was
only briefly married to a phony Polish prince.

"The art of life is salvage," I said to Jessica Phillips, one
valiant afternoon when she'd volunteered to help me scrub
water stains out of some murky chintz chairs. And though
it sounded like something Princess Radziwill would say, it
seemed like a sorry truth to me. From what I'd seen so far,
much of adult life was a struggle to make a ruined thing

that much better; to repair, and patch, and glue back together again. And for people like Jessica—who never seemed to mind when, after a day of hard scrubbing, a floral print was only slightly less blotted—incremental improvement was satisfying. Sometimes, it was even hard to say which Jessica preferred, a stain or a stain-remover.

But I hated both.

I hated the grime spot on the wingback chair that looked like Australia, and that no afghan, however artfully draped, would ever conceal. And I hated knowing that no matter what I did—and no matter what arcane, simmering, lethal solution Jessica purchased from the all-night Wal-Mart— the spot would never entirely go away. Of course, I wished that every stick of furniture I owned hadn't been stuck on the back of a flatbed truck in the midst of a freakish downpour. But if Jesus had ordained the spoiling of my worldly goods, I'd begun to wish they'd been spoiled completely, and burned to ash. "Half a loaf really *is* worse than none," I told Jessica, squeegeeing solvent off the sides of her mop bucket, and damning The Land Down-Under with all my might.

"Wrong," she said. "Half a loaf is a lucky day."

I, however, was unconvinced. Having failed at lunchmeat, I simply couldn't bear more shame or disappointment, and the very idea of applying for another job was enough to make me flop-sweat. Determined to prevent anything odious from happening to me again, I decided that if I couldn't win, I'd drop out. Which prevented *anything* from happening to me, and ground my life to a cranking, screeching halt.

After the Honey Ham Sandwich Shop, I spent most days with my feet on the dashboard of Mother's car, riding back and forth with Michael to his classes at the state university. As he studied, I snuck Cokes into the college library, and read Nancy Mitford novels barefoot in shadowy corners barricaded by books. "It's disgusting!" Mother roared over the phone. "All you do is follow Michael around reading little books!" Which was terribly unfair of Mother, because I also went to a lot of lunches—where the courses crept and the gossip sprang—with whatever resilient lady would take me.

And all the resilient ladies took me to lunch from June 1997 to June 1998—The Year When Nothing Happened—in order to tell me, each in her way, that I was squandering my youth. And because she had a constitution like a duck's back, it was Tina Marie who mostly paid my tab. Tina lacked patience for my Honey Ham woes. "After all," she insisted one afternoon over Japanese, wiggling her toes as we sat cross-legged, sipping green tea on silk cushions, "my career as a nurse ended when I was eighteen, and look at me now. It was all for the best. Who knows? If not for being cruelly fired from that hospital, I might never have made it in the theater."

I doubted that, since the whole reason Tina had been cruelly fired in the first place was because anyone could tell—even, eventually, her colleagues in the trauma ward—that Tina Marie wasn't really a nurse. Tina was an actress. However, she'd once played a nurse in summer stock, and when the show closed, she stole her costume from the wardrobe room. Then, between acting gigs that fall, she'd sweet-talked her way into the office of an employment agent who, terrifyingly, took her résumé on faith, and placed her at work in an Upper East Side hospital—where she went undiscovered for a good six weeks before rather messily gauzing a gunshot wound, and being stripped of her stethoscope.

"I feel like this is a different situation," I told Tina.

"How is this a different situation?" she asked.

"For starters, you were never really a nurse."

"And you," said Tina, "were never really a ham-glazer."

Though she coached from a different medium, Tina Marie also suggested I consider my life material: "You are a character in a play yet to be written," she said. Tina extended her arms, like she was tap-dancing on the inside. "And there are only three questions keeping you and Michael from being a smash hit. One"—Tina made the one sign with her index finger—"who are you? Two"—her finger- and toenails were painted exactly the same color— "what's going to happen to you? And three"—that color was Jungle Red—"who the hell cares?" Sometimes when Tina gave advice, you could almost hear the orchestra swell.

But there was no music to my grandmother's tough love. JoAnn was as dramatic as Tina, but she tended to downplay live theater in favor of the silver screen. "You want to talk unfair?" she asked me one afternoon, as I monkey-climbed the warehouse shelving of a dodgy clearance outlet, in a quixotic search for the perfect goosedown pillow: firm, but yielding, and very, very cheap. All the pillows I'd pitched onto the polished concrete floor had been positively disillusioning, and JoAnn was getting grouchy. She squeezed through a stack of pillows with contempt, and I made the mistake of answering a rhetorical question. *"Polyfill!"* JoAnn shouted. *"Feather blends!* Christ, Robert, when are you going to stop acting like a child, and accomplish something?"

"At the moment," I replied, "I am attempting to redress the bitter unfairness of my life." This was insensitive, I know. Particularly in light of JoAnn's foiled pursuit of quality bedding.

"Let's talk about unfair, you and me," said JoAnn. She clutched a pillow in each hand, and squinted into the halogen lights. "Let's talk about Gene Tierney. Or better yet, Frances Farmer. What do you know about Frances Farmer?"

"I saw the movie," I mumbled. I hoisted myself to a higher shelf.

"Well, then, let's talk about having a lobotomy. *In Oregon*. And getting molested in a state home. And having Kim Stanley for a mother! After you've been a gorgeous blond movie starlet. So admit it, Mr. Quiet Desperation, compared to that you don't have it so bad, now do you?"

"I admit it," I said. "Compared to Frances Farmer, I don't have it so bad."

"I *thought* not," JoAnn hissed.

"Coming down!" I cried, and tossed two more pillows, of apparent good breeding, to my grandmother's feet.

In the months since I'd asked JoAnn for money to flee Mrs. Rayburn and escape to Kay of Elk, JoAnn and I had founded a relationship based on love and bargain shopping. During that phone call, while explaining the urgency of transferring high schools, I'd told JoAnn I was gay.

To which her response had been even more unsatisfying than Mother's.

First, silence. "Hello?" I asked.

"Oh darling, I'm so sorry," said JoAnn. Her voice was rushed and awkward. "It's just that . . . didn't we already know that? What I mean to say is . . . I thought everybody was already sort of working on that assumption."

Just once, for the sake of variety, for the drama of disclosure, it would be nice for *somebody* to react with surprise when I tell them I'm gay. After all, one of the nicest parts of being gay is that you're born with a great conversation starter, and it's a real mood-kill when *everyone* reacts as though you're reading from yesterday's newspaper.

Then JoAnn asked me, "Have you ever read *P.S. Your Cat Is Dead?*"

And after I said that I hadn't, she suggested a number of other books by James Kirkwood, and I told my grandmother I was in love with a beautiful man named Michael Leleux.

"*Leuuleuuu?*" She sounded like her mouth was melting. "Isn't that the French skunk on TV?"

"No, that's Pepe Le *Peu*. Michael is a Le*leux*."

"Wait a minute. Say the skunk again."

"Le *Peu*."

"And what'd you say Michael's name was?"

"Le*leux*."

JoAnn snorted. "There's not one lick of difference, and you know it."

But when JoAnn actually saw Michael, a different kind of melting process took place. "My God," she cried, grasping Michael's face in her hands like she was reading him in Braille. "Young man. You have Ava Gardner's dimples." This was entrée, since JoAnn, by her own admission, had never really recovered from not having been Ava Gardner. Afterward, Michael and I began receiving invitations for cold suppers and old movies at JoAnn and Alfred's house. One evening, while JoAnn and Michael were in the kitchen, my grandfather latched onto my elbow: "This is what I have to say about Gay," he said. He squared me with a low nod. "Better a man than a Yankee girl."

In late spring, we saw *Some Came Running*, and JoAnn toasted us over blue crab, "You two are the next Martin and Lewis!" Which was really very sweet, because just try and think of another marriage between men.

"We're the next Martin and Lewis," I said. "Except we have sex."

"Pass the salt," said JoAnn.

CHAPTER EIGHTEEN

Loose Lips Sink Ships

Michael made a prized pig of himself over our new relationship with JoAnn and Alfred. He wallowed and gloated until he grew positively gouty with swollen pride, and I rolled over in bed with *The Last of Chéri*. "You said a reunion was impossible in your family," Michael said. Propping himself on his side, even his muscles looked ready to burst. "Remember that? You said it would take a miracle. Then you said you weren't even sure a miracle could swing it. Because Jesus could bring back Lazarus faster than he could resurrect your family. Does any of that ring a bell, Robert?"

I put down Colette, and glared at Michael like he was a philistine. There's a real hardship to being quotable, and that's that people tend to remember exactly what you had to say on a subject.

"But here's my real question," Michael carried on. "Do you think ... in your own personal opinion ... would you and I be enjoying such caramel-y goodness, such mashed-potato-like relations with your grandparents, if I weren't so undeniably adorable?" Michael ran his fingers through his hair. The hair glistened.

I glowered, and thought that if our bed was a temple, Michael would be a moneychanger.

"How about calling your father?" he asked. Michael scooted closer to snuggle, and I shrugged him away. "I think this might be the ideal time, don't you? Maybe you're on a lucky streak? Let's brainstorm estranged relatives you can drop a line to."

"Have you suffered an aneurism?" I asked Michael. "Have you recently developed thrombosis? The one thing we don't need in this whole world is *more* family. I think somebody's going to have to put a shunt in your head, because we're full-up with relatives, you and me. So until one of them drops dead, there's a No Vacancy sign in the window."

In the summer of 1998, Mother came for a visit. My parents' divorce was—finally—over, except for a stack of unsigned documents, to which Mother might have attended through the mail, if she hadn't also been desperate to visit the Evangelical plastic surgeon. And the reason Mother was in dire straits to acquire a doctor's care was because there's nothing, apparently, as filthy, contaminating, and bacteria-ridden as an old lipstick tube—a warning she'd received on the day of her lip implantation, but which had gone, tragically, unheeded. And now, because Mother was too cheap to toss away her old lip-gloss, and, in particular, had clung to one perfect shade discontinued by Guerlain, neither of the incisions in the center of her lips (through which tiny silicon wedges had been stuffed like garlic into pork roast—two in the top lip, a longer one in the bottom) had ever healed properly. By now, Mother had battled low-grade infections for well over a year. Milky green puss oozed out of the holes in her mouth, and throughout the day, gradually melted away her lipstick.

Admittedly, Mother's bottom lip was worse than her top. As each day passed, it looked more like a tennis ball, while the top lip had, eventually, taken its own initiative in purging the source of infection. First, it fermented, or something very much like it. And then one morning, when fog settled over the Bay like nagging doubts, and Mother gently dabbed at her puss with a wet wipe in the ladies' lounge of the Intimate Apparel department of a major San Francisco clothier, she watched in horror as one of her top lip's implants bottle-rocketed out of her mouth, and with a resonant slap, collided with the opposite wall.

Mother called me from the parking lot. "You think you know public humiliation. You think you've met shame. But you haven't. Not until your little rubber parts start falling off in the middle of a department store. Not until you know what Gumby feels like."

"You mean you weren't alone?"

"Of course not. I mean, why would I have been? God really had to plan that one, and He wanted an audience."

"What happened?"

"Not much, actually. Small children wept."

"Children?"

"Twins. With their young mother. I'm not sure, but I think my implant might have, ever so slightly, grazed the rosy apple cheek of one of her little girls. I don't think any actual pain was involved, but, well, I think the appropriate word is traumatized."

"Oh my God. What did the mother say?"

"Well, Robert, what was there to *say*? She was mortified. Struck dumb. Rendered speechless. She looked at me like . . . well, like my infected lip implant just shot her child. There's really no adequate metaphor."

"Then what happened?"

"Well, the twins were wailing. And I just kept telling their mother how really, truly sorry I was to have been . . . the potential catalyst of . . . years of intensive psychotherapy for her two little towheads. And at the same time, I was searching madly around the floor, trying to find where my goddamned implant landed, so I could take it back to that sorry doctor, and show him just exactly what he's done to me. But it wasn't easy, because I'm wearing heels, and this skirt's on the snug side. So I was having a lot of trouble bending and squatting, and I didn't want to step down too hard, because I just knew I was going to squish it. And when I finally did find it, lodged between the wall and the hinge of a stall door, the twins' mother made what I consider a very Christian gesture, under the circumstances. She handed me a Ziploc from her diaper bag. So I could keep my implant fresh in my pocketbook. She never said a word. She just stuck her arm out, and handed me that baggy. And then I said thank you, thank you very much, how sweet, sweet, sweet, and then I apologized some more, as I slowly backed my way out the bathroom door. Carrying my ejected lip implant with all the dignity a lady can muster."

"Oh, poor Mother," I sighed.

"It's enough to make a girl start believing in inner beauty," she said.

Mother preserved her discharged implant—grass-green and rancid—out of a sense of violation. And though she was desperate to have the other two removed, she walked around for months with a lopsided mouth, curled into a sort of Elvis-ian snarl. Because she refused to pay for a California doctor's treatment, and insisted on waiting instead for her return trip to Houston to demand restitution, in the form of de-implantation, potent antibiotics, and a saline flush from the Evangelical plastic surgeon.

Despite her gruesome errand, I couldn't wait to see Mother. It had been nearly a year since her last trip to Houston, and I didn't expect to face difficulty in tempting her away for some seafood and shopping between appointments. Because even before losing her lip implant in the ladies' room, Mother had complained bitterly about San Francisco department stores: "Everything's *sage green* here," Mother ranted, a rant only slightly mitigated by the fact that her mouth didn't quite come together right. "And all that talk you hear about San Francisco being The Oasis of Culture in the Old West? Well, it's bullshit. None of the women here do a thing with themselves! Not so much as a stitch of makeup. And nobody has a hairstyle. Only hair*cuts*. It's like they're afraid of distracting from their precious view. San Francisco is the only city in America where the boys are prettier than the girls."

But, on the July morning of her arrival, Mother's flight landed during the onset of another of Houston's day-long monsoons, and idle shopping was out of the question. After watching the Weather Channel, Michael's mom wrung a Kleenex wad at the very idea of our driving to the airport. But "*Après moi le déluge,*" Mother joked, as she kissed our cheeks outside baggage claim. Michael pulled onto the freeway, just as jungle rain began splattering the windshield. Mother was lithe in a white pantsuit that almost made her look tan; and she kept a cocktail napkin pressed to her mouth, and leaned between our seats so she could squeeze our shoulders and talk close to our faces. Which was lovely, because I'd missed my mother terribly. But her affection was ill-timed. As the hot rain poured, the car steamed like broccoli, and in the heavy air, the awful odor of Mother's lip infection spoiled my hopes for lunchtime shellfish.

Ever since the soaking of all my earthly goods, I'd been a little panicky about rain. A determined drizzle was enough to put me on edge, but what Michael was maneuvering Mother's Jaguar through, while slowly winding our way to her lawyer's downtown office, was a downright flood. The car was too low to wade through the fast-rising waters on the Interstate, and Michael was trying to chart a path of higher ground through a shoddy series of inner-city neighborhoods. "Goddamn it to hell!" Mother hollered from her perch between us (and honestly, I don't know how Mother managed to keep food down with that gamey smell of infection right under her nose). "Goddamn it to fucking hell! Everything's so goddamned extreme here!" And while Michael and I wiped steam off the windshield with our shirt sleeves, Mother pulled out her lighter, and began puffing a menthol.

Upon occasion, Mother complained that living in San Francisco reminded her of an episode of *The Wild, Wild West* in which a man dies, and is sent to a heaven that is drippingly gorgeous, but also so unbearably dull that, eventually, he realizes he's rotting in hell. I was capable of understanding Bland as a form of torture, and sometimes I felt sorry for Mother, because she was as fierce and rowdy as Texas. And on a given day, living with an almost-astronaut in a beautiful house overlooking the ocean could be enough to make you peel your scalp off. However—as Mother's cigarette smoke filled the foggy car, chugging and sputtering through standing water, and the stink of to-bacco mingled with the stink of infection; and Mother poked Michael and yelled, over the pounding of rain on the roof, "If you don't drive faster, we'll never make it! And *understand* me, Michael. I cannot live through another summer's day with these implants. When I go outside, the buzzards fly lower"—I looked at Mother and realized I couldn't tell if she was snarling or not, and began to con-sider that extreme people are, perhaps, better suited to bland climates, and that it's possible most Texans should be exported.

We arrived at Mother's lawyer's office just as he turned out his lights. The bayous of Houston were pooling, and employers were emptying downtown's tall buildings, sending their staff home while the roads were still drivable. But Mother pushed her way through the door, and as Michael and I stood dripping on a Navajo rug, she used one hand to move a ballpoint pen through a pile of papers, signing lines as her lawyer pointed to them. And with the other hand, she telephoned her plastic surgeon, tossing threats like lit matches and berating him for succumbing to mass hysteria by even considering slinking home before fulfilling his Hippocratic oath: ". . . I don't care if you have to *snorkel* home, my mouth is luring birds of prey . . . well, you just better be there . . . well, if I can get there from San Francisco, then I'm sure you can make it from River Oaks, okay?"

When Mother's lawyer stopped pointing to dotted lines, she said, "That it?" He shuffled through her divorce papers like poker and said, "Yep. That's it." Then the lawyer grabbed his umbrella, and Mother grabbed her handbag and started herding Michael and me through a heavy oak door, whittled and chopped to look like kindling twigs and branches. "Get a move on," Mother told us. "Water's rising."

So ended my parents' marriage.

By the time we arrived at office number 305, with brass crucifix gleaming, the Evangelical plastic surgeon had, of course, flown the coop. Mother kicked and pounded his locked door so hard Jesus rattled on the cross, and then she rushed us down to the lobby, where she screamed into a pay phone at his answering service. Then Mother did something far more sinister—she cupped her hand over the telephone receiver, glanced over her shoulder at Michael and me, and whispered.

I don't know what Mother said to that answering service.

But whatever it was must have been worthy of J. Edgar Hoover, because when I asked her to repeat it, she shook her head, and (who knows?) snarled. Then she straightened her suit jacket, and said, "The doctor will be right back." And—in the time it took our elevator to ascend to his third-floor office, and for Mother to grind half a dozen cigarette butts into the dull, speckled carpet—her plastic surgeon did indeed materialize, looking vexed, and as though he'd swum the bayous.

Michael and I sat in the dim, chrome-accented waiting room I'd visited two years earlier, on that day I'd believed my mother's vagina was hemorrhaging, while the Evangelical plastic surgeon performed a brisk procedure that sounded like agony, but which significantly improved Mother's odor.

The only unfortunate thing about Mother not being enveloped in a cloud of her own stink was that it enabled her to discern, and then complain about, other smells. That night, for instance, after Michael forded the freeways back to his parents' house, where Mother had been invited to sleep in the guest room, she wouldn't stop complaining about how bad the house stank of soup. "And not even quality soup—this place stinks like cheap, canned, noodle-y soup, Robert. It's being absorbed into my very pores!"

Michael's parents' house didn't *quite* smell like soup—it smelled like gumbo. There was really no hope of it not being absorbed into your clothing, and yes, into your pores. On any day, the wallpaper held the aroma of years' worth of Mom's gumbo roux, but that evening, in particular, the whole house was hazy with it, because of the special, company gumbo Mom had gone to efforts to brew on Mother's behalf.

At dinner, Mother looked positively wheezy, and not just from gumbo. Like the lobster in the boiling pot, I'd grown slowly accustomed to the lethal caliber of the Leleuxs' chitchat. I usually read fashion magazines at the dining table, but sometimes, I made an effort to engage Michael's relatives by telling amusing stories—except the stories they found most amusing were those that made my family sound crazy; stories about things like my mother's infected lip implants bullet-spraying small children. But since Mother was actually present that evening, the party was dependent upon the table talk provided by Michael's sister and brother-in-law, which put a real damper on things. For most of the meal, Michael's sister told a story (and not for the first time, mind you), about Mountain Dew at her CCD class. "Can you believe," she asked, "that one of the mothers actually brought Mountain Dew and doughnuts for refreshments? The doughnuts I don't mind, but everybody knows Mountain Dew has more caffeine than just about any other kind of coke you can think of. My dog knows Mountain Dew has more caffeine than any other kind of coke you can think of. It has more caffeine than Coca-Cola, and it has more caffeine than Pepsi, and it has more caffeine than Dr. Pepper, and it has more caffeine than Mr. Pibb. She could have brought ginger ale, and she could have brought Sprite, and she could have brought Slice, all of which have no caffeine. Or she could have brought juice, or she could have brought Kool-Aid, or she could have brought Hi-C. She could have brought milk, or even plain old water. But she didn't. She brought Mountain Dew. And I could hardly believe it. I mean, can you? Can you hardly even believe it?"

Then Michael's oldest sister's husband said he didn't even like the taste of Mountain Dew.

Then Michael's mom said she didn't think she'd ever tasted Mountain Dew.

Then Michael's dad told her it tasted sort of like Sprite, and sort of like Irish Spring soap.

Then Michael said he could have sworn he saw Mom drink a Mountain Dew at Skyler's birthday party at Cici's Pizza Parlor.

I didn't say anything, because I was reading an article about the history of Harris tweed, and also thinking that, all in all, I hadn't come very far from Nana and her pancake-powder biscuits. And Mother didn't say anything either, because somewhere around Mr. Pibb, her eyes glazed over, and she lost consciousness. And by the time Mom served Coke floats, Mother had excused herself from the table, explaining she needed rest after the day's trying surgical procedure.

Mother had been mysterious about the length of her stay in Houston. She'd stressed her need for spontaneity when I'd inquired as to when Michael and I would be returning her to the airport. So I was devastated, though not surprised, when, the next pearly morning, Mother had her bags packed in the Jaguar by the time I awoke, and told me she couldn't even stay for couche-couche, another

Cajun delicacy Mom was making for breakfast. That wasn't the devastating part. Devastation awaited: "Let me wake up Michael," I told Mother. "He'll just die if we head off to the airport without him."

"Well, honey pie . . ." said Mother. (Honey pie was the first shoe dropping.) "That won't be necessary."

"What are you talking about?" I said. "If you fly off without kissing him good-bye, he'll be absolutely crushed for life."

"Sweetie baby, that's not going to happen."

"You mean you don't want to tell Michael good-bye?"

"No, I mean I'm not flying home."

"But what do you mean?" I'd once been told that soap opera stars, when they've forgotten their lines, are trained to say "But what do you mean?" Frequently, Mother made me feel like a stumped soap star. Like I had the IQ of a mold spore.

"I'm driving home."

Mother hadn't slammed the trunk completely closed. Its hood was bobbing, ever so slightly, in the morning breeze.

"Sugar-pop," said Mother. "I *need* my car in California. Peter drives his roadster, and that means I'm left driving the gardener's truck most of the time. You don't want Mommy driving an old, stinky gardener's truck, now do you? It doesn't even have a muffler, and it's covered in potting soil."

"I suppose it's your car," I mumbled. It *was* Mother's car, but it was my last remnant of wealth. Without it, Michael and I would be stuck with his parents' spare car—a practically pre-Mesozoic Chevrolet Impala, which had been a

Pennzoil company car before Dad retired, and was only a hairsbreadth smaller than the H.M.S. *Britannia*.

Mother reached out for a hug, and toppled towards me. "Tell Michael I love him," she said.

"Of course," I said.

"And you know I love you." If Mother squeezed me any tighter, my blood vessels were going to pop.

"At the moment, I'm only fair-to-middling about you," I said.

"You'll recover," Mother said.

Then she slammed the trunk, climbed into the driver's seat, and idled under the magnolia tree in the Leleuxs' yard for a moment. Then she rolled down her window, and signaled for me to come closer. And when I did, Mother took the bracelet off her wrist; her last piece of real jewelry, with diamonds and emeralds clustered like daisies. Mother dangled the bracelet towards my hand, and then closed my fingers around it. "Hock it, honey," she told me. "Get yourself an apartment. Get yourself any place that doesn't smell like soup. Christ, I don't know how you've borne it as long as you have." Then Mother kissed the hand she'd wrapped around her bracelet, and waved, and backed the car away, and blew a kiss, and drove off.

Two years earlier, when I'd been certain I was losing Mother, her jewelry seemed holy. Every stone she sold felt like a little sparkly piece of Mother traded for money. But this July morning in 1998, when Dad's grass was just starting to shrivel and wither from the crackling dog-day heat, and the exhaust from Mother's car lingered in the air like a tulle skirt, and I finally turned to walk into the house, I caught a glimpse of the Impala (which really was of an adequate proportion for a family of Cubans to safely drift onto Miami Beach), and could hardly wait; I counted the very breaths I inhaled before I could wake up Michael, and drag him to the nearest pawnshop.

CHAPTER NINETEEN

Do I Hear a Waltz?

*S*ee a palace rise from a two-room flat, due to one little
word—Married": That's how the song goes, and I was
singing it in August 1998, when, after merrily hocking
Mother's bracelet, Michael and I rented an apartment with
barely two rooms on Angiers Street in Huntsville, Texas,
mere minutes from the Sam Houston State University
dance department. Our new home was the front half of a
forties bungalow, choppily subdivided by our golden-
locked landlord—an aged adolescent in thigh-high boots
who spent his days sculpting what looked like placentae
out of what seemed like paper clips, and otherwise in-
dulging himself in the privileges of having inherited half
the town. The bungalow buzzed with termites, so the very
walls seemed in the midst of a disappearing act; and you
didn't so much open our front door as you picked it up and
carried it; and the musty old floors pitched to the left, so
walking from the icebox to the toilet felt like sailing rough

waters; and twice, in the single year we lived there, Michael took a foolhardy step, and tumbled through the floor. It was a dump. It was paradise. I've never been so happy in all my life.

The first morning I woke up there, tangled in the new cream-colored sheets (stiff as canvas) I'd bought from the discount store, with a torrent of late-summer light fanning the floor in little shadow-strips from the Venetian blinds, I kissed Michael good-bye on his way to dance class. For breakfast, I got myself a Coca-Cola from the Frigidaire—bulging and old-fashioned, like a marshmallow with a long, chrome, crank handle—and in my cutoff jeans, I un-packed my encyclopedias from the cardboard liquor boxes Michael got free from Randall's grocery store. Then, after settling my books on an improvised shelf above the kitchen cabinets, I sat Indian-style in the icy, delicious wind of the rattling window-unit, sipping my Coke. The record player clanged the score from *Around the World in Eighty Days* as I polished each of the least water-damaged pieces of Mother's furniture we'd chosen as decoration for our sweet hovel. And if St. Peter had me pick one radiant moment, a single bright-haloed second of living bliss, I'd choose sitting on my own floor, with a Coke and a bottle of Lemon Pledge, and Michael coming back to me any minute. I could have sworn the window-unit was blowing joy onto my back.

Michael and I moved to Huntsville in the last weeks of its summer snooze, before several thousand students returned for the fall semester. For the moment, swans brazenly pranced about the public park—dappled with blossoming trees and whitewashed fences—without fear of being trampled; and Café Texan and King's Candies and the antique shops lining town square yawned empty of customers. None of Huntsville's dawdling citizens seemed able to stand upright in the wilting heat—they leaned against shop counters, or collapsed into folding chairs, and slowed to a sort-of tumbleweed pace. But despite this—and though the heat climbed to 112 that August, and the plastic seats of our mammoth Impala burned the hair right off the back of my legs—I could hear a thrilling rustle in the town, like the sound of ice cracking on a thawing river. Or the hooves of the horses pulling the stagecoach round the pass. Our life in Huntsville—the whole, honeymooning year of it— felt on-the-cusp, like we were the first two people in the movie theater. At first I thought it was just because school was starting, and young life was returning to a country town, but later I noticed I still felt like something wonderful was just about to happen to me. That September, Michael and I went to the Harris County courthouse, and stood together before a judge—in the only way we could contrive to go to a courthouse and stand together before a judge—and changed my name to Robert Leleux.

But there were those upon whom the charms of our new life were lost: everybody.

I'd always assumed the expression "burst into tears" was figurative, but that was before we invited Michael's mom and dad to Huntsville for dinner, with the mind-boggling purpose of actually showing off our new home. When Yvella Leleux walked through the front door of our apartment, it was less like crossing a threshold than it was like breaking a membrane. In a movement that began in her stomach, Mom's entire body convulsed. Gripping her handbag to her chest, tears sprang from her eyes, and a French wail from her hanging mouth. And since Mom had reverted to French, Dad started speaking to me in English: "The reason," Dad said, "I worked so hard all my life was so I'd never have to see my son living in a place like this." He gave me a look like I'd lured his son into the gutter, and Michael and I made a split-second decision to eat out that night.

But Mother's criticism was broader. She spoke darkly into the telephone. "You mean to tell me, you sold my gorgeous diamond bracelet to move to *Huntsville*? Where the *prison* is?"

"Huntsville is a sweet little town. And it's cheap," I said. "And Michael's almost finished with his degree, anyway. So it's only temporary."

"Huntsville is not a sweet little town, Robert. It's a place where they chicken-fry people. It's a place where the lights flicker at midnight."

"You're exaggerating," I said. "It's been lethal injection for years now, and you know it."

"As your mother, it terrifies me that you're missing the point of this conversation. But tell me, Robert, would you say that Huntsville, Texas, is the best place for a gay couple to be living?"

Well, this was a very good question, but one I was hard-pressed to answer. I'd always dreamed of moving away from Texas. But I'd never been happier in my life than I was in Huntsville—even though I knew, in such a place, there was no future for me as a writer, and to Mother's point, Michael and I did stand a fair chance of being lynched. And while *politically* I believed in Having It All, romance had served me so well, I didn't want to seem grabby. My life was practically pastoral, and I was afraid to push my luck. This, despite the fact that Huntsville was a complicated place, and in ways I'd tended to overlook, having spent most of my time there in a state of love-rapture. The whole town, for instance, was supported by the government—through either Sam Houston State University or the prison. And at many points, the two institutions adjoined—in a literal, property-line sense, and through Sam Houston's Criminal Justice department, where most of the prison administration was educated, and, most apparently, in the town's culture. I'd been told, for instance, that the starting salary of a prison guard was, dollar-for-dollar, that of a beginning university professor's, and both institutions issued paychecks on the same day. So on the first of the month, the grocery store swarmed with academics and security guards.

While playing house with my True Love, grateful to be in a town where not one of our relatives lived, I hadn't imagined the swans roving under the mimosa trees, but I had ignored the prison's death chamber. Which was no small feat—because, in addition to killing more prisoners annually than any other such contraption in a Western democracy, the death chamber was also a macabre source of local pride. "Old Sparky," the town's retired electric chair, was preserved at the Prison Museum. As a genuine tourist attraction, it was advertised in visitor's bureau pamphlets, and depicted as the centerpiece of a mural in the town's shopping mall. Shortly before we moved to Huntsville, a concert performed by Michael's dance department coincided with the lethal injection of axe-murderer Karla Faye Tucker. That night, a police officer was stationed at one of Huntsville's main intersections: "This way to the modern dance concert," she waved one white-gloved hand, "and that way to the execution."

I tend to be a navel for quirk, so it's hard for me to generalize about a group of people—but, by and large, Huntsvillians did seem a little peculiar. Deep East Texas peculiar. That fall, I met a prison guard named Daisy, whose dream it was to quit lockdown in order to become what she called a "colonic therapist." Meaning she dreamt of installing an enema booth at The Facemaker, the local ladies' beauty parlor, in order to provide a sort of one-stop shopping experience to Huntsville's Old Guard as they sat waiting between their pedicures and permanent waves. Another woman, named Jeanette, longed to find employment at the women's prison since her husband, a former Houston neurologist, suffered brain damage when a bowling ball fell on his head as he cleaned the garage. And, most peculiarly, Huntsville, Texas, seemed to be the only place in America where I spoke with an English accent.

Or at least, where I was popularly confused as speaking with an English accent.

My voice had always had a buttery drawl that tended to slip extra vowels into simple English words, and slowly spread them across syllables. But never, in my entire life, had anyone ever mistaken me for British.

Except in Huntsville, Texas. Where, from those first logy August weeks, stooped countryfolk started speaking to me with the assumption that I hailed from London, England. "It must be so hard," said a woman with hair as white and tightly rolled as a cotton boll, "living here, so far away from your family."

Thinking she must have confused me with a university student, studying far from home, and wanting to be polite, I replied, "Yes, thank you. It is hard."

Then the old woman clucked her tongue. "To think, a nice young man living all the way across the ocean from his family."

This was confusing.

But not for long, because it became a mistake so common that I soon began to expect it.

"You're a long way from London, England, aren't you, son?" asked one craggy-faced cowboy whose skin had absorbed the color of chewing tobacco.

"I am a long way from London, England," I said. "But I'm from Houston, Texas."

The cowboy eyed me warily. He leaned back onto the heels of his boots. "I've been to Houston, Texas," he said. "And that *ain't* the way people talk there."

But why would anyone lie about coming from Houston? I wondered. If I were going to lie, I'd say I *was* from London, wouldn't I?

Well, eureka.

As it turned out, pretending that I was from London turned out to be a mighty fine idea, serving as both free entertainment and a time-saving social strategy—particularly during the first anniversary of the tragic death of Princess Diana, over which the matrons of Huntsville, in a showing of grief for my fallen princess, fell into line to offer me their respects. And on behalf of my queen and my nation, I nodded to each, "Thank you, mum."

Everybody found this hilarious in the fall of 1998, and especially our newest best friend, Michael's dance professor, Dr. Cindy Gratz, a sort-of Groucho Marxist who had the gift of taking nothing too seriously. Everybody that is, except my grandmother JoAnn, who thought I was wasting my time and talents mocking the yokels. In general, there wasn't much about my life in Huntsville that JoAnn found funny. Sure, Mom and Dad had gotten hysterically French after they'd taken the plunge and come to dinner, but my grandparents refused to even visit our apartment. And JoAnn was so appalled by our car that she wouldn't even park next to it in her butter yellow Cadillac. Now, I was certainly no fan of my '84 Impala—it had no air-conditioning, was held together by duct tape in the way some people are by religious faith, and made a kind of rattle-rattle thumping sound that grew deafening when you drove faster than forty-five miles an hour—but it was still, I argued with my grandmother, more to be pitied than shunned.

But in October 1998, when another tragic death occurred, that of Matthew Shepard in Laramie, Wyoming—a rural, western, university town bearing a spooky resemblance to Huntsville, Texas—JoAnn stopped finding my life not-funny, and grew downright fretful, and then did what people in my family tend to do in times of strife.

She went out to lunch.

JoAnn invited Tina Marie, The New Jessica, Dr. Cindy Gratz, and me to join her at a hushed and mirrored Houston eatery. Under normal circumstances, the fact that my women friends hated one another was a source of great pain and feminist frustration, but in this particular instance, I was grateful for anything that forestalled conversation. Because though my grandmother referred to this as a friendly luncheon at the Empress of China, it was truly a constitutional convention for the ladies who loved me to confer upon the topic of my terrible choices.

Until JoAnn called the meeting to order, no one spoke above a smirk. You could hear the rustling of the tablecloth, and the sound of tea being poured into tall glasses. I was the only person at the table to deliver my lunch order, sweet-and-sour chicken, to the waitress in an audible voice. (I always ordered sweet-and-sour chicken at the Empress of China, for the reason that it reminded me of my family—it wasn't the greatest, but at least I recognized it on the menu.) Then my grandmother clanked her knife against her iced-tea glass and, smiling benevolently, said, "The reason I've invited you all here today is because, to my grandson's ear, my voice sounds like a windshield wiper. But it seems possible that you ladies might be able to persuade him to go away to college—since, let's face it, he's not getting any younger, and the bloom is off the rose any day now, and I'm fairly confident that remaining in Huntsville, Texas, he'll meet Jesus being dragged behind a pickup truck." I took a deep swig of tea, and thought that in order to get away with a speech like that, JoAnn ought really to have been wearing a hat. "Any thoughts, ladies?" JoAnn asked.

But she didn't have to ask twice, because on the topic of the likelihood of my impending murder, JoAnn found general agreement. "I never say good-bye to Robert without wondering if this is the day his big mouth gets him bound and flayed," said Cindy.

"I feel so guilty asking him not to speak out loud in public," said Tina.

"Sometimes he doesn't even have to talk," said Jessica. "I mean, the paisley pants."

"My God," Cindy said. "The paisley pants."

"Even if we ignore the probability of violent death," Tina told me, "Huntsville, Texas, is still not the place for a young writer."

"New York is the place for a young writer," said Cindy.

"Unless you want to write country-western songs," said Jessica, "and then the place is Nashville."

Tina took off her sunglasses, and settled down to business. "What plans have you and Michael made for life after his graduation next May?" she asked.

And I said that while, of course, Michael and I always talked about moving to Manhattan, I really wasn't sure what he wanted to do.

Which elicited a collective groan from the table, and particularly from JoAnn, who made a sound under her breath like she was trying to find the pitch. "Don't get me wrong, ladies," she said. "I love Michael. I love Michael's dimples. But it just seems to me that all my grandson does is follow him around reading a book. Now, I adore my husband.

There's not a day that goes by when I don't thank the Lord for Alfred Wilson. But, darling," JoAnn turned to me. "Not only is a good man hard to find, a good man is not enough. The people in my family, our strength hasn't proven to be balance and moderation. My mother. My *daughter*. Robert, you've got to have something to do with yourself. Trust me, darling," said JoAnn. "Ugly things happen to people who don't fulfill their potential." My grandmother gestured as though she were opening a fan. "You've got to spread out," she said. Which caused her to mention Betty Friedan, and The Problem That Has No Name.

Which reminded Tina of divorcing Dick the Draper and her triumphant return to the stage. "You've got to have a gimmick," she told me.

"Have you given *any* thought as to where you might want to go to college?" Jessica asked.

"NYU or Columbia," I said. "Then again, I've always dreamt of being the first boy to integrate Smith."

JoAnn looked at me like her hair hurt.

I ignored this. "Then there's Sarah Lawrence," I said.

I liked the idea of Sarah Lawrence because of its writing program and radical politics, and because it was a commutable distance from Manhattan. And JoAnn liked the idea of Sarah Lawrence because it sounded like the ladies' finishing school of her dreams. And Cindy liked the idea of Sarah Lawrence because Martha Graham used to teach there. And Tina said that while studying with Stella Adler, she'd known several artsy Sarah Lawrence girls, all of whom had excellent nose jobs. And by the time my sweet-and-sour chicken arrived, I'd promised my grandmother

I'd at least fill out an application to Sarah Lawrence for the fall of 1999.

JoAnn telephoned that night: "Darling," she said, "tell me your favorite color."

"Lavender," I said.

"For large rolling metal objects."

"Like lawnmowers?" I asked.

"Sort of," said JoAnn.

"Blue," I said.

"How do you feel about butter yellow?" she asked.

"Not so much," I said.

"That's all I need to know."

I rolled over. "Michael," I said. "I think my grandparents are planning to buy us a lawnmower. Either that, or a car."

CHAPTER TWENTY

Sons & Lovers

Four months later, I was gripped by Ronald Firbank near the ROTC cannons at the entrance of the dance department, idling with *Vainglory* in the periwinkle-blue Chevrolet JoAnn had given us for Christmas, and waiting for Michael to emerge from his Labanotation class. We had shopping to do, because the previous evening Jessica Phillips had come to dinner with her boxer, Fallon Carrington, who'd lapped up the scraps of an iffy batch of sugarfree banana instant pudding, and as a result, had eaten the Venetian blinds right off the bedroom window during a fit of leaping, gastronomic madness. Jessica was mortified, and insisted on pushpinning the doggy towel from her pickup into the window frame, which looked unbearable, and if anything, drove us faster into the purchase of a new blind-set.

Nevertheless, before we hit the discount store, I insisted on swinging by the bungalow to check the mail, because the Sarah Lawrence admissions office had sworn to deliver a final decision by the middle of March. It was now the thirteenth of March. For the past three days, our postman had refused to deliver our mail, and had instead penned wounded notes to our neighbor Jolene, who rented the back half of the bungalow and often obstructed the mailbox with her Cutlass Supreme. Jolene was a single mother to whom men were always writing wounded notes: They were the tears and she was the pillow. I often had sympathy for her, but in the final days of awaiting my (God help me) acceptance letter my better self was tried and I wanted my mail.

I'd at first applied to Sarah Lawrence at my grandmother's urging, which was shortly followed by Michael and Mother's urging, and also because of JoAnn's dark implication of the existence of a sinister relationship between the filing of my college application and my receipt of a large rolling metal object for Christmas. But in the months since, I'd begun to hang myself upon the hope that this funny little college might say yes to me. I'd sent them some poems, along with an essay about adoring Michael and my longing to become a writer in a town where Christian witness was scrawled onto the bathroom walls, like For a Good Time Call Jesus and I'm not kidding. And one January day, Jessica had driven Michael and me to a Houston hotel to meet Sarah Brice Lynch, a college recruiter who joked that everybody at Sarah Lawrence was forced to change their name to Sarah, and who seemed to be the kindest, most sympathetic person I'd ever met.

By early March, I'd scored a suspense-induced form of delirium tremens: I jittered and prickled, was flu-ish with worry, and couldn't shake two competing sets of images. The first set involved Michael and me moving to New York City in the fall, and greatly resembled the opening sequence of *The Mary Tyler Moore Show*. And the alternate set involved me working at the Huntsville Wal-Mart for the rest of my life—a fate which, at the moment, the U.S. Postal Service seemed to be conspiring to fulfill.

However, when I pulled into our driveway, Jolene was bottle-feeding Baby Jack by the azalea bush on our front porch, and waiting to deliver a bundle of our completely worthless mail. Along with another, taller piece of information. "Hey, Robert."

"Hey, Jolene," I said.

"Your letter didn't come, hon."

Because this was too important a question to leave to Jolene's trust, I shrugged the inky rubber band off the stack and flipped through it myself. But Jolene was right.

"Shit," I said. "I feel like I live at the end of the world. I feel like those dreams where you yell and yell, but there's no sound. I feel like that song about the Alamo where the people never came never came never came."

Michael cleared his throat.

"Well *somebody* came for you," said Jolene.

"For me?" I asked. "Who?"

"Your father."

"Wrong," I said. "You mean Michael's father. Old, ornery, rosary, smelled like soup and nitroglycerin tablets."

"Nope. I mean your father. Tall, tan, bald, muscle-y. Looked like one of those awards they give the movie stars."

"The Oscars," Michael gasped.

"Did you actually speak to him?" I asked.

Baby Jack wriggled like a basket of puppies. Jolene swatted at his tiny fingers as they danced with the buttons of her blouse. "Oh, honey, I talked you *up*. I told him about Michael's graduation and your little blue car and that Sarah Lawrence letter coming any day now. He's real sweet, Robert." Then Jolene made the kind of frowny face you drew at the end of a sentence when you were in the second grade. "But he's also real *sad*. All he could talk about was how much he misses you. He wanted you to know that. That, and how bad he wants to meet Michael."

Another wounded note.

"Then it couldn't have been my father," I said. "My father is a bastard who abandoned his family for a pregnant jockey."

"He even showed me a Father's Day card he keeps on his dashboard from when you were five years old. It said Happy Father's Day. With sweet little hearts and an XX and an OO. I just think it's something how you can tell so much just from the way somebody's child writes just that, XX and OO."

"What I think is something is that living less than a mile from the state penitentiary, you opened your door to a complete stranger. A completely bald complete stranger. Who could have been anybody. Who could have been the Texarkana Killer for all you knew."

"Well, he had a Father's Day card, Robert."

"Jolene was just being nice, Robert," said Michael.

Now, Michael is perfect in every way. But when your spouse is having a fight with somebody, here's what I

244 | The Memoirs of a Beautiful Boy

think. I think that if you only have something nice to say, it's better to say nothing at all. But for the moment, I ignored Michael, and stuck with Jolene. "I bet you even gave him a Dr. Pepper, didn't you?" I asked.

"It was a *very* hot day," said Jolene. She was struggling to stand, but with Baby Jack in her arms, the effort took a couple of elephant heaves.

"Please move away from my azalea bush," I said.

"He cried, Robert. Your own father. The man sat right down at my kitchen table and cried like a little baby."

"I don't care if he gurgled and cooed. Thank you for dropping by now, Jolene," I said.

"I can't believe you're kicking me off your front porch because your father knocked on my front door and I didn't turn him away."

This wasn't quite right, since Jolene lived in the back half of the bungalow and technically didn't have a front door.

"You'll have to excuse Robert," Michael said. "He's just a little hungry right now."

Baby Jack's bottle clattered onto the porch, and he started wailing and grasping for it.

"I am not hungry," I said. "I'm sick of being told I'm hungry all the time."

"He gets like this when he's hungry," said Michael.

"What I have is a headache," I said. "I have a headache, and I don't have any aspirin because I don't have any money, because my father left my mother and me to have babies with Seattle Slew."

Jolene was bouncing Baby Jack, trying to hush him, and

keep him from reaching his filthy bottle. "So you do know he's had a couple more kids."

"What?" I asked.

"Well you said bab*ies*. You said he left you and your mother to have babies with Seattle Slew. He didn't think you knew about the second one. That you have a little baby sister *and* a little baby brother."

Michael looked at me like I'd caught The China Syndrome. "Jolene," he said. "Robert and I were on our way to the store anyway."

"They named the girl Grace after Princess Grace, and they named the boy Nolan after Nolan Ryan."

"We were really just stopping by for the mail," said Michael.

"Robert," said Jolene, "your daddy left something for you." She started to reach into her back pocket.

"Is it money?" I asked.

"It's a letter," she said.

"Then you can keep it," I said.

"You mean to tell me you don't want to read your daddy's letter?"

"I'd love to read it, but I just washed my hair."

"Why don't you just stick it under the door for now," said Michael.

"She can stick it somewhere," I muttered.

"Something I noticed . . . ," said Jolene. She'd crammed Daddy's letter into the doorframe, just above the knob beneath those tiny metal hairs that keep the door from slamming too hard. Baby Jack was climbing Jolene's shoulder, and she was just about to round the corner of the house. I was staring at my sandals and counting my toes. And Michael was reeling from his codependent's dilemma, trying to decide who to comfort. "Michael and your daddy," she said—this was her parting shot—"they have the same sweetness. I don't know if you've ever noticed that before. But it's hard to believe you hate your father so much when you married somebody just like him."

"Lady," I said. "From now on you better watch where you park your Cutlass Supreme."

"Okay. So Jolene didn't show good sense," Michael said hours later. Hours after he'd placed my body into our new periwinkle car, and driven me to the discount store, where he'd purchased our replacement blinds alone while I stared out the window, and hours after he coasted me around Huntsville, and out to the state park and back, while I sat still and quiet. One thing that takes years to learn when you're a naturally loud person is that nothing you could possibly say to the people who love you is as terrifying as silence. Not that I was absolutely silent. I did answer Michael when he asked if I was okay, and then if I was sure I was okay, and then, that even though he knew I wasn't really okay, could I please clear my throat every once in a while because he wasn't used to this much peace and quiet and he wanted to make sure I was breathing. But hours afterward, late that evening, Michael said, "Even though Jolene showed lousy judgment, I still think this is the very best thing that could have happened."

"*This* is the very best thing?" I asked. "In my whole life, this is the most I have to look forward to?"

"Of course not," said Michael. "What you have to look forward to is being admitted into Sarah Lawrence and moving to Manhattan and becoming a famous, successful writer and then living happily ever after. But what I mean is, that in order for you to actually be happy during happily ever after, you need to resolve this thing with your father, and I think that this is the only way that would ever be accomplished."

"Have you been dipped?" I asked. "This is the most humiliating way for this to be accomplished. Knocking on doors, and crying and weeping and carrying on with my next-door neighbor. It's harrowing. You tell me, how am I ever going to be able to look that woman in the face and condescend to her ever again?"

"If I ever lost you," said Michael, "I'd knock on doors."

"And if you ever left me," I said, "you could cry me a river." Which is exactly what this whole situation felt like. Like "Cry Me a River" or "Some of These Days," or any of those big boa-ed songs about the sweet, sweet pleasure of slamming the door right in the face of the man who done you wrong. Except here Michael was trying to ruin everything by pouring cold water all over my righteous indignation. And besides that, Daddy wasn't playing fair. I hadn't had the chance to slam my door in his face, because it wasn't even *my* door he'd knocked on! Daddy was soliciting recruits. Before I knew it, he'd established a groundswell of popular support. It was disgusting. There were rules to groveling, and so far, he'd broken every one. "I'm furious with my father," I said. "I hate my father."

"I don't care how you feel," said Michael. "I just want you to grow up and show a little gratitude."

"Have you been drinking the thermometer?" I asked him. "Has modern dance joggled your little brain? What do I have to feel grateful to my father for?"

"What do you think your life would be like today if your father hadn't fucked around and left your mother? Who, by the way, has never been happier in her whole it's-better-to-look-good-than-to-feel-good-darling life. And how many years and years would it have taken you to pry yourself away from her if the shit hadn't hit the fan in this particular way, if in fact you ever would have, since you two had a serious *Sweet Bird of Youth* thing going on between you."

"*Suddenly, Last Summer*," I said.

"The one where the gay guy gets eaten in the last act."

"That's the one," I said.

"And speaking of," said Michael, "do you really believe you would have had the guts to fall in love with me if we'd met before your family fell apart? Living out on the ranch with the O'Dooles in Petunia? Which, need I say more, is another significant opportunity for gratitude. And do you think your father would be so thrilled to meet me now, if he weren't just desperate to get you back in his life? Or that you'd have ever even applied to Sarah Lawrence, much less been accepted. Much less been awarded enough scholarship money to move to New York City and become a writer."

"Those last things haven't even happened yet," I said.

"They will."

"So you're saying I should thank my father, whom I hate, for leaving me?"

"I'm saying it never could have happened any other way."

"You're only saying that because this is the only way it ever did happen."

"What I'm saying is, they're the same thing."

Then Michael got up for a glass of water. It seems to me that this is exactly what you get for growing up dreaming about not-marrying Dashiell Hammett. You get an older man who's much better looking than you are, offering enigmatic counsel that sounds a lot wiser than it actually is. And if I didn't like it, then I had only myself to blame. Myself and Lillian Hellman.

It also occurred to me that Michael's whole notion of The Greater Good was so Catholic in a way I couldn't quite put my finger on. And though it's not a theological position, it crossed my mind that there's just something about Catholicism that promotes a real you-can't-make-an-omelet attitude toward history—that all's well that ends well, the ends justify the means, and gee, It's a Wonderful Life. While to your average Protestant, I would say the means matter a great deal. I would go so far as to say that the means were what the Reformation was all about. But I was distracted from this idea by the thought of *It's a Wonderful Life*, Daddy's life parable, which reminded me of Jolene's last, revolting snipe—that my father reminded her of Michael—which was truly, up until that moment, the most repulsive idea ever to scurry across my brow.

And that's when Michael walked back into the room—not with a glass of water, of course, but with Daddy's letter. *Dear Son,* Michael read.

"How'd the bastard ever find me anyway?"

I'm sure your mother told you about my asking her lawyer for your address.

"It's the Ides of March," I said. "And my enemies surround me."

I saw this in the newspaper, and I knew you'd laugh. Love, Daddy.

"What's he talking about? What did he see in the paper?"

"A Charlie Brown cartoon," said Michael.

Michael handed me a comic strip. It was about the girl with the naturally curly hair. I searched for metaphorical significance: There was none. I started to tear the cartoon into tiny confetti pieces, but then noticed Daddy had written his phone number on the back. Michael saw me hesitate. "Hand me the telephone," I said.

"You're going to call him?" asked Michael.

"No, I'm going to call my mother," I said. First I called Mother collect, because I figured that if I was yelling, she should pay. But Peter answered and refused the charges. So then I called back long-distance, and this time Mother answered. "I can't believe you gave Daddy my address!" I yelled. "Without even asking me! Without even warning me!"

"Did he give you any money?" Mother asked.

"He gave me a *Peanuts* cartoon," I said.

"Well, I would have sworn he'd have given you money," said Mother.

"Are you kidding?" I grunted. "In order to get money, I'd actually have to speak to him."

"How much do you think you'd get?"

"You *are* kidding," I said.

"Because I wouldn't pick up the phone for less than a thousand."

"Mother," I said. "I'm not picking up the phone at all."

"Let me talk to Michael," she said.

CHAPTER TWENTY-ONE

Next Year in Jerusalem

The fact that Michael predicted my acceptance to Sarah Lawrence, as well as my scholarship, and proved himself practically clairvoyant when it came to my future, did little to cut the excitement when two days later, on March 15 precisely, I received my admissions packet in the mail. I carried the envelope into the apartment feeling my brain slosh about my skull, and like I was walking on the moon. And gripping Michael's knee with one hand, I slowly peeled the paper back with the other. Here's how the folder's cover read: "*A wave of light breaks into our darkness, and it is as though a voice were saying . . . You are accepted. You are accepted.*"

"Jesus," said Michael. "Imagine what they say to the ones they've rejected."

For the next month, all my stars aligned. Mother and Peter finally set a wedding date in late November, an occasion to which Michael and I would fly from Manhattan, where we would then, blessedly, be living. And Jule Jo Ramirez, Michael's best friend from his last stab at New York, heard tell of an August vacancy in her apartment building. The rent was walloping, but in an optimistic spasm, Michael and I joined hands and jumped, waving off our money worries until later. All the while, Michael bustled through his final college semester, choreographing a brand-new piece for the senior concert and dancing in two others.

"What do you want for your graduation present?" I asked Michael in early April. He was writing an American literature paper with devil-may-care haste and a sangfroid that I, at the time, associated with a real mastery of the material. "China, crystal, or silver?"

One of the worst things about not being able to marry Michael was that we never had a wedding, and one of the worst things about never having a wedding was that we didn't get any wedding presents. However, I'd been recently struck with the idea of parlaying Michael's graduation into an opportunity to rake in all the engagement party–wedding loot we'd missed out on by registering at a department store, at the same time providing our friends and relatives with the chance to stand proudly for social equality through the purchase of fine linens and kitchenware. I couldn't help myself; I'd been positively mired in Virginia Woolf ever since my admittance to Sarah Lawrence—which I figured to be the kind of place where no one did a thing but sit around talking about Virginia Woolf all day, and I'd better bone up now or humiliate myself later. Consequently, I was now capable of turning stemware into a political debate. "If we were a straight couple," I'd lectured Michael for weeks now, "all our friends and family would have bought us the pattern of our choosing. And you and I wouldn't, now, be relegated to eating off my mother's old hand-me-downs. Doesn't that seem blazingly unfair to you?"

Michael shrugged. "I like your mother's plates," he said. "They're nice. I like the blue flowers."

A little choking sound emitted from my throat. "The point, Michael, is not whether you like blue flowers or you don't like blue flowers. The point is a china service of one's own."

But it had been impossible to interest Michael in this conversation, mainly because, as I discovered on that April day he positively breezed through his paper on nineteenth-century poetry, Michael was advocating his own platform. "Well, whatever you want," I told him, "you'd better decide quick. Because if I don't tell Mother and JoAnn soon, you'll end up with a Dopp kit and then that'll teach you to take our civil liberties seriously."

"What I want," said Michael, barely glancing away from the computer, "is for you to invite your father to my graduation ceremony."

Since his March 13 visit with Jolene, Daddy had courted me. Three more comic strips arrived in the mail: *Hagar the Horrible, Beetle Bailey, The Family Circus.* I was a hunted man. Life in our Huntsville love nest was no longer serenely tucked away. I never knew what telephone call, or knock on the door, or batch of mail might signal an end to my peace. Now I longed for Jolene to barricade the mailbox. I decided I wouldn't feel safe before landing at La Guardia, and asked anyone who would listen what the world was coming to when a young man was run out of state by his own kith and kin? As far as I was concerned, the phone could ring off its hook, but Michael leapt for it every time. "Why are you intent on spoiling our one opportunity to cash in?" I asked him. "When you know this is our chance to get anything we want?"

"But this *is* the only thing I really want," Michael said.

"Of course it is," I said. "Because you're warped enough to ask for the one thing you know I'd refuse to give you."

"You mean to tell me," he asked, "that knowing that the only thing I really want is for you to call your father, you still wouldn't call your father?"

"This is not a conversation in which I'm denying you something," I said.

"You know what I find ironic?" Michael asked. (I just thought it was quiveringly impressive the way Michael could deeply consider Emily Dickinson and banter at the same time. Especially since it had taken me weeks of hushed, heavy labor to finish my Sarah Lawrence application essay.) "What I find ironic is that for going on three years, I've listened to you complain about your father abandoning you, and now suddenly, you're complaining about your father coming back. I think maybe you just get satisfaction out of having an outraged story to tell. I think there must be some people who just like being angry."

"What a disgusting thing to say," I said. And tossed my head back.

"You asked *me* what *I* wanted for *my* graduation," Michael said. "And what I want is for you to call your father."

"Well, if I were you," I said, and having already tossed my head back, I found myself at a loss for an adequate gesture, "if I were you, I'd start browsing for china patterns." Then I got on the telephone with Mother and JoAnn, and told them Michael's heart was set on Haviland.

But by May all my organizing was for naught. Michael wasn't getting any graduation presents because Michael wasn't graduating because Michael flunked American literature with a resounding thud on account of the wantonly crummy papers he'd dashed off throughout the spring semester. Which meant we'd be moving to New York without a degree, or a place-setting, between us, and Michael would have to retake the class by correspondence next fall, because like most people (Dashiell Hammett included) who gave terrific advice, he made frequent stinking decisions when it came to his own life.

When Michael started college, the Berlin Wall stood like Gibraltar. He'd been a now-and-then student for so long I'd begun to suspect that his reluctance to graduate represented some kind of pathology. And now that he stood at the very brink of a BFA, he'd managed to give it the slip one more time. I was furious—because the plan was for Michael to support us in New York and that plan would have benefited from a bachelor's degree. But I was even angrier that, through sheer recklessness, Michael had spoiled the perfect dovetailing of our Texas life. "If this were a book," I complained, "this would not be the way this book ends."

Michael insisted the six-month delay of his modern-dance degree would not be the thing to sink us in New York City, and that as far as the end of stories went, rough edges were like beauty marks.

Though I was somewhat persuaded, I found that having begun to worry, I couldn't stop. Through a tiny snag, real life wormed its way into my plans for the fall. It suddenly hit me that moving into a Manhattan apartment—even the apartment Jule Jo had found for us, which was practically a garret and from a quality-of-life standpoint was on a fairly even keel with our hovel on Angiers Street—was going to cost thousands. Unless I wanted to wind up wedged in the bowels of Queens—and I was absolutely, I'd-rather-be-pulverized, *not* moving to Queens, because Decent is closer to Heinous than Wonderful, and I would, in such a case, rather live in Lubbock—the time had come for me to invent some cash.

Well, the obvious solution was to sell our beautiful blue car. It was a luxury in Manhattan and no matter how I worked the numbers, our immediate future didn't look luxurious. But then, my grandparents had just bought us that car, specifically and misguidedly for our new New York life (I don't think either of them could quite conceive of being publicly transported), and if there was any way around it, I wanted to avoid seeming ungrateful. It made my gums ache to give Michael too much credit, but he'd been right about JoAnn and Alfred—when I wandered into their refrigerator, I could stick my hand into the pickle jar; I could forget to refill the ice trays, or fall asleep with my shoes on the couch. And though such actions placed my very life at the mercy of JoAnn's left hook, I knew I'd never be unwelcome. There was a slow, seeping comfort to that, just as there had been at Michael's parents'—like settling into a down cushion—that had come to seem fundamental and precious.

So, selling the car was our last resort. Of course, Michael's mom and dad were ruled out for reasons of wherewithal. And since the car had been their contribution to our move, I couldn't ask JoAnn and Alfred for money. Tina Marie and Cindy had both thrown us dinners, and for months Jessica Phillips had collected her pocket change in jelly jars for a Bon Voyage fund. The only person left was Mother, who was fresh out of hockable jewelry. Mother continued to send as much money as she could spare, and was filching more every time Peter averted an eye, but the rest of her cash had to be funneled into her wedding plans. Daily, she Federal Expressed cake samples and white silk swatches to Huntsville requesting my opinion, and my forgiveness for failing to offer more help. "If it comes right down to it," Mother told me, "I suppose I could pawn Peter's engagement ring. But I'm sure he'll notice it, darling."

By Independence Day, I'd begun to think I couldn't afford a scholarship.

By Bastille Day, I could barely look our car in the headlights—I felt I could count its life in hours. Patting its periwinkle hood, I apologized: "You and me have had us some good times," I said. "But between you and New York City, New York City wins."

And then one day, just a week before the absolute last day Jule Jo could hand her landlady our first and last month's rent, and a security deposit, a sum that altogether amounted to well over a year's rent at Angiers Street, I went to the mailbox and discovered a *Kathy* cartoon.

"Think of it this way," said Michael. "Your father owes you."

"You're not fooling me, Michael," I said. "You think you've found the chink in my armor. You think you can turn my refusal to live in an outer borough to your advantage. But you can't. Because I'm not living above 125th Street, and I'm not calling Daddy."

"You're not going to like what I have to say to you," said Mother over the telephone.

"You're going to say you think I should call my father," I exhaled.

"I think you should call your father," said Mother.

"Why don't you call him for me?" I asked.

"Because I'd rather eat my own teeth," she said.

"But you're fine with me calling him," I said.

"During Vietnam, Lyndon Johnson used to say, 'I'm the only president you've got.' "

"You're saying that Bob O'Doole is the only father I've got."

"Yes, and for that, my darling, I truly do apologize,"

Mother said. "But Bob O'Doole will not be the only husband I'm going to have. And sometimes in life we have to
make little sacrifices for the sake of money. Sometimes we
have to cleave off little bits of our dignity in order to further ourselves. Some of us have to wear pom-poms on our
heads. And some of us have to face disgrace by losing our
silicone implants in public restrooms. Some of us have to
sell every last scrap of beautiful jewelry we've collected in
exchange for marrying men we never loved, who aged to
look just like the Academy Award we've always wanted
but know we'll never win—all in order to take care of our
beautiful sons. But, lucky for you, my sweet baby, because
Jesus has marked you for a special, special plan, you don't
have to marry anybody you find, quite frankly, unhygienic.
You just have to call your rat-bastard father. And if he
doesn't give you any money, then you can tell him to go
fuck himself."

"Fine," I said to Michael. "You win. I'll call my father. But
I want you to know that the only reason I'm doing it is for
the money. And because I believe Jesus might be bargain-
ing with me—everything I want, for the one thing I've
refused to give up."

"I couldn't care less about your motivation," said
Michael. Which, again, was just so Catholic of him.

"Hold my hand," I said.

I took *Kathy* out of my wallet.

I turned the comic strip over and dialed the telephone
number written on the back. "Hel-lo," Daddy said. Just like

that, with the inflection rising in the middle like a swing set. If you played the guitar while my father spoke, you'd have a country-western song. His voice had a hangdog sweetness—slow and heavy and pained, like his words were being filtered through Karo syrup. I almost hung up the phone. Michael squeezed my hand harder. The blood in my temples rushed, like I'd had too much caffeine. "Hello . . . ," I said, because I didn't know what to call my father. I hadn't spoken to him as an adult, and *Daddy* seemed icky for a grown man. "It's . . . me," I said.

"Hello, darlin'," he said. "Gee, I was starting to think I might never hear your sweet little voice again."

Which, right off the bat, was provoking. Because if this phone call was a song, I was determined not to let it be a love song. "Well, until this minute, I wasn't sure you'd ever hear my sweet little voice again, either," I said. I wanted to make it clear to Daddy that he wasn't going to be able to just waltz away with me. That whatever intentions he might have for this conversation, I owned it. It was my phone call, and even if I'd only made it for the money, I still wasn't going to sell myself away.

"I know it, darlin'," he said. "I know it. I'm sure there's a lotta things you'd like to say to your daddy. And I sure want you to have the chance to say them."

I sighed. Because when you've hated someone like I'd hated Daddy—for years, and so much so that little trickles of spittle formed at the corners of your mouth every time you devised some new axe-wielding, limb-by-limb method of hacking him to death—finally hearing his voice again can really undermine your concept of good and evil, especially when that voice is sort of sweet. Nauseating, but sweet. This was the reason Mother should have been making this phone call—because instead of fighting you, Daddy had a way of co-opting your argument, of absorbing it through agreement, or even offering a more extreme version of your own position. Daddy was Paper, and Mother was Scissors; she could always handle him. But even as a child, I had to hate Daddy from afar—because I always chose rock, and Daddy covered me every time. And I never knew what to do about it.

I started to cry. "I'm still so furious with you," I told him. Between the two of us, *I* was the wounded party.

"Sure you are, sugar. I wouldn't blame you if you hated me," he said. All the sad, country sounds were in Daddy's voice—coyotes and train whistles and tears in beers. It was so perverse of him, usurping my right to sound pitiful. He should have sounded grateful, chipper even, that I'd deigned to call him.

"I do hate you," I said.

"I know it," he said. "I'm just so glad you're calling me." I put the phone down for a second because I didn't want him to hear me crying, because I knew I couldn't stand to hear him comfort me. I clenched my teeth and scowled at Michael. For the moment, I hated him, too. Michael was also crying, and the hand he was holding had gone numb.

"The only reason I am calling you," I said, "is because I'm moving to New York."

"It's where you've always wanted to be," he said. And at that moment, more than Daddy or Michael, I hated myself—I was melting. Because there was something in

Daddy's voice that, I swear, must have been biological, that just plucked my heart like a bow. Or rather, goddamn it, like a guitar. And it was vulgar and cheap and such lousy writing.

"I only called you for the money," I said. There was nothing short of hanging up that I could do to keep him from hearing me sob. "I can't wait to get out of this god-forsaken place."

"Whatever I can do to help," said Daddy.

"Well, it better be plenty," I said, but I'm not quite sure he heard me because by this point I was practically heaving.

"You've always been so special. Such a special person," he said. "You and your mother. There's never been a day in my life, not one day ever since I was nineteen years old, when I wasn't completely in love with your mother and you. That's been my whole life," he said. Which is, I think, the single most disgusting thing anyone has ever said to me. That Mother and I were special enough to get walked out on. Michael was holding me, so I pinched his arm until the skin twisted, and I only wished it were possible to spit on somebody through the telephone. Only the high cost of Manhattan rents prevented me from hanging up.

"Oh, really." I coughed. "And what about Pam? Is Pam a special person, too?"

"Pam's been real good to me," he said. Like he was the tiredest man in the world.

"Daddy," I said.

"What about lunch," he said. "With Michael."

"Tomorrow," I said. "Luby's Cafeteria."

"I love you, angel," he said.

"Bring your checkbook," I told him. Then I hung up the phone and rattled my head and made bubble-gum motions with my jaw because I'd somehow managed to cry into my ears.

"Say something!" said Michael. And because my ears were wet, his voice sounded furry. Michael narrowed his eyes. "He wasn't mean to you?" he asked.

"Worse," I said. "He loves me."

Encore! Encore!

The night before Michael and I left for New York, we met Tina Marie at the playhouse. She was in the last throes of staging a musical revue featuring an equal number of solos to cast members. Which was a number that now exceeded forty, because this was a benefit for the Fireman's Association, and Tina said a person with a solo will *always* sell more tickets than a person in the chorus, and who cares if the show lasts four hours if it helps to prevent one fire.

Tina had invited us to midnight breakfast after rehearsal, but she'd also asked for Michael's help in setting "It's To-day," which was her own solo in the revue, and came from the first Roaring Twenties scene of *Mame*, where she dances on the piano in a sequined pantsuit. But Tina had just starred in *Mame*, and wanted to wear the louche gold sari from the finale, for which she'd paid a ransom. It was more flattering than the pantsuit and twinkled brighter in the lights—but, unfortunately, made it impossible to dance on a piano and had absolutely nothing to do with the Roaring Twenties.

These were to be Michael's principal choreographic challenges.

And while he faced them with what I thought considerable flair, since there are only so many dance steps appropriate to a torch song performed in traditional Indian garb, I became more, and then more, melancholy, as I was suddenly struck with something like buyer's remorse.

The more exultant Tina's singing, the less it seemed as though Michael and I were heading for New York, and the more it felt like we were leaving Houston forever. For the first time I thought that someone would have to maybe be crazy to move nearly two thousand miles from the place where people loved him. So, by the time the playhouse cleared, and Michael and Tina were hungry for pancakes, I was almost in tears because it seemed possible that I was a person who couldn't enjoy a good thing while it was happening, and who would never be entirely at home in this place or that, but would, instead, always be pacing between rooms.

Tina was still in the gold sari. Which was about as good for climbing stairs as it was for piano dancing. So she asked me to help her up to the technical booth to turn the lights out, and the second time I stepped on her kick pleat, Tina swung her skirt up, and asked what the hell was the matter with me.

"Nothing," I said.

"Robert," said Tina.

"Nothing," I said.

"I'm going to start singing any minute now," she warned.

"I'm just afraid of how much I'm going to miss all this," I said. "Because I already miss it, and I'm standing right here."

"So you'll come back," said Tina.

"But what if I can't? What if I'm never able to come back, and things aren't ever the same, and I won't ever be where I am right now?"

"You have to come back," said Tina. Tiny gold flecks of her makeup were getting all over my sleeve. "You have to come back because next summer, in particular, I will need your help."

"My help," I said.

"Well, you're a writer, aren't you?" she asked.

"I suppose so," I said.

"And by next year you'll be an even better writer, won't you?"

"That remains to be seen."

"Well, what's certain is that I have a new musical planned for the summer."

Tina and I were almost at the top of the stairs. But her pace seemed to be slowing as she vamped the scene. "Go on," I said.

"A *premiere*," she said. "Just picture it." Tina waved her arm. "The musical version of . . . *Star Wars*. Of course, we'll never get the rights for it, so I'll call it *Galactic Battles*!" Which made Tina wave her arm again. "An original score. With original lyrics. And that's where you come in,

Robert, because what the hell do I know about writing lyrics?"

We'd finally reached the top of the stairs. "And for Michael? Imagine. A light-saber ballet. All in the dark."

DARLINGS, SUFFER THE GRATITUDE

First and always, two people.

For my mother, The Great & Indomitable Jessica Wilson, who gave me life and material, and who not only knows how to take a joke, but knows how to write one, too. There's not a word in this book she hasn't inspired, and then improved upon with her wit and smarts and style. When the answering machine picks up my telephone, the first thing Mother says is, "Pick up the goddamned phone." But the second thing she says is, "Listen darling, I've had the greatest new idea for The Book. It came to me in a dream . . ." My mother is my movie star and my football hero, and nothing feels impossible when she charges forth, mink coat abristle. Of all the women in the world, I would choose her for my mother. No child or man has ever been luckier than I.

And for Michael Leleux, love-of-my-life, who made me human and happy. You know the story in the back of *People* magazine, about the woman who buys the Rembrandt for five bucks at the garage sale? Well, that woman was me, and Michael's my Rembrandt, and there's not a day in my life when I'm not astounded by the treasure of him, and my own dumb animal luck. Not many people receive the blessing of being married to the best person they ever knew.

And, of course, for my father and his family. My father is so kind and sweet, and I love him dearly. When I showed him an early version of this book, here's what he said, "I'm so proud of you. You've really become what you set out to be. You're a real writer. But, I just can't read any more of this." I mean, is that a great guy, or what? Generous.

For my unbelievably gorgeous, marvelous, and heart-strung grandparents, JoAnn & Alfred Wilson, who've shown me what it means to love one person forever. My grandmother JoAnn is the original, and I've become an artist by setting her self and style to paper. And wedding party or no, my grandfather, Alfred Wilson, is always the best man. His first job was as foreman on his grandmother's cotton plantation for chissakes, and today he calls to ask whether I've finally gotten around to that article in *The Nation*. I adore them both, and my life would be empty and meaningless without them.

For The Women Who Loved Me—Jessica Phillips, Tina Cafeo, Cindy Gratz, Marilyn Bellock, Ello *(He had a hat?)* Black, Joanna Friesen, & Jule Jo Ramirez—for unreasonable, unyielding, unflagging, and undeniable friendship. You've given me love and gossip and money and food, and a home wherever I wander. My life's great irony is that I am a ladies' man.

For Marie Howe, Paul Lisicky, Honor Moore, Victoria Redel, Donna Masini, Jan Heller Levi, Eva Kollisch, Jane Cooper, Edward Swift, and Jean Valentine—who made me a writer, and gave me the world of New York.

For my great-grandmother, Eugenia Dennard Peacock, who started the whole damn thing.

For Yvella & Chester Leleux, who gave me their life and home and son and family—out of love and sheer, caramel-y goodness.

For Kay Curtis, who showed me what it means to be an artist, and a thinker, and a good, good person.

For Peggy Curtis, who is no shrinking violet, but who is a steel magnolia, a bed of roses, a fair flower of Texas maidenhood, and a garden all her own, and who, with bright-eyed Jimmy, has given us one big happy family.

For Keri Schmidt & Kim Broom, who've proven that it's possible to be happy and kind and beautiful and funny and sober, all at the same time.

For Betty Fleming & Kathryn Ross, who are deep in my heart while deep in the heart of Texas.

For Suzanne Gardinier, Julie Abraham & Amy Schrager Lang, Rose Anne Thom, Sarah Brice Lynch, Thyra Briggs, and Heather McDonnell, who gave me a mind of my own.

For Sarah Lawrence College, which gave me an education, a wing, and a prayer.

For friendship real and true: Inan Howe, Andrea Eisenstein-Winard & Yosef, Donnette Heath, Harriet Hodges, Diane Cates & Gene, Scott Wright, Manny Cafeo, Christoph Keller, Sharon Pilotta, Heather Milliet, Nadia Ackerman & Rich Frankel, Darrell Pucciarello, Naomi

Replansky, Ila Gross, Elena Brancato, Peggy Lasut, Sigrid Nunez, Michael Klein, Charles Flowers, Glenda Leleux, Susan Levine, Maggie Rouen, Gary Esposito & Marisela & Dante, Benedicta Otalor, Patrick Horrigan, Humberto Alers, Mauricio Londono, Priscilla Lang, Jessica Bennington, and Amira Gertz.

For Skyler Morgan, Madison Quinn, Kylie Quinn, Jessica Selph, Angela Tauzin, Christopher Sikes, and Jasmine Sikes. Each of you is like a favorite painting at the Met, in which I always see one beautiful new thing.

For Joanne Brownstein, whose boots were made for more than walking.

For Henry Kaufman and Laura Plattner.

For Blair Chymberjehle, who could never see anything more beautiful than herself.

For Gorgeous George Witte, who is like the GPS in your car—a certain, soothing voice who always knows how to get there, and never yells if you're too stupid to listen.

For Gail Hochman, who is a faith-based initiative unto herself, and is, in every wonderful way, a young Streisand.

For the most Hon. Sissy Farenthold, who, as the song says, shines forth in splendor, and makes me proud of where I'm from.

And in memory of Mark Edward, Ann Richards, and Molly Ivins, three great gals from Texas.

THE MEMOIRS OF A BEAUTIFUL BOY

by Robert Leleux

About the Author

- A Few Words from Mother
- A Conversation with Robert Leleux
- "Bedecked" by Victoria Redel

Keep on Reading

- Recommended Reading
- Reading Group Questions

For more reading group suggestions
visit www.readinggroupgold.com

ST. MARTIN'S GRIFFIN

For nearly thirty years, **Robert Leleux** has remained internationally unknown as a celebrated bon vivant, fashion icon, and man about town. Neither the best-selling author of *Highland Fling* (1931) or *Wigs on the Green* (1935), Mr. Leleux's work is in no way associated with that circle of Bright Young Things who illuminated the London social scene during the inter-war years. He is known not to have been portrayed by Julie Christie in John Schlesinger's Oscar-winning film *Darling*, and does not currently reside at Swinbrook House in the Cotswolds.

Credit: Michael Leleux

A Few Words from Mother

To the Readers of My Genius Son's Book,

Everywhere I go with Robert, people ask me,
"Don't you mind the things your son writes
about you? The wigs, the plastic surgery, the
vomit..."And my answer is no, it doesn't bother
me that Robert writes about it, it bothers me
that I had to live through it.

Most of the events Robert recounts in this book
occurred during the most god-awful time. And
though, in looking back, I can see that much of
my behavior was, well, unusual, it all seemed so
reasonable at the time. Which brings me to
another thing people tend to ask me when I'm
out with Robert:

"What have you learned from the experiences
you've lived through?"

And my answer is "Nothing." "Nothing?"
they repeat. "Well, I wouldn't shave my head
again." Because that really wasn't a good idea.
But again, at the time, it seemed entirely logical.
Which tends to be the way with life. It seems
you can operate with complete certainty, and
still, in the long run, be completely wrong.
Shit. Wrong and stubborn really is a terrible
combination.

But of course, you don't know that until
much later. Sometimes not until your son
writes a book about it. And that, in its own

way, is a marvelous consolation, because at least something good and funny came out of the lousy times.

At least Robert can see the humor in the really terrible decisions I made, instead of just silently resenting me for them, like the children of every other woman in every other country club in America. As it turns out, I've had bad luck with all the men of my life, except my son. There hasn't been a single moment of his life when I haven't worshipped and adored Robert, and now there's a book to prove it. With a beautiful picture of us on the cover. Heavenly.

Much love,

Jessica Wilson (Mother)

A Conversation with Robert Leleux

*Excerpted from an interview conducted by
Kelly Hewitt at www.loadedquestions.blogspot.com*

Is there any part of your writing that you attribute to a life growing up in the Lone Star State?

The Mouth of the South, my grandmother used to call me. And as for Texas, I dearly love it. Houston is home for me in a way that no other place ever will be. I might be alone in this, but I actually think it's a beautiful city, and every time I go back, something in me just sings. And I believe that East Texas is just about THE best place in America for a writer to come from—because it hasn't yet succumbed to that horrible homogenization of language that's stripped so much of America of its regional sounds. It seems to me that there's only a handful of places left that sound like themselves, and I think that maintaining that is so precious. Grace Paley said something like, "a writer has to listen to the world with two ears: one turned to the language of literature, and the other turned to the language of the street you grew up on." And it's so terrific to have been born to a place where the language is so charged and funny and off-kilter gorgeous.

A few reviewers have warned readers that your book is "not for the faint of heart." Do you think that's a fair label?

What's the expression? "Faint heart never won fair maiden." Something like that. Well, I don't know—practically everyone in Michael's family has a heart condition, and they all loved my book. And there have been a couple of completely lovely ladies who've written to say that they read my book in the hospital, and that they laughed so hard, their nurses thought they were having some sort of attack, and what do you know, laughter really is the best medicine. Which absolutely makes my life worthwhile—the opportunity to actually cheer up a person who really needs of a good laugh. Who could ask for anything more? I mean, the magical, miraculous thing about books is that you write them alone, in an empty room—a really private experience—and then, they venture out alone in the world. They enter rooms you'll never see, they meet people who'll forever be strangers to you. It's very moving to me—especially since my book's a memoir, and there are people out there I'll never know, with whom I'm having this very sort of intimate experience. VERY strange, and wonderful. But to answer your question—if you want Barbara Pym (AND I love Barbara Pym), I'm not Barbara Pym. Or as Joan Crawford said, "If you want the girl next door, go next door."

What was it like doing your book tour with your mother?

Well, I maintain that it's a real marker of virile masculinity, traveling with your mother. How many brawny He-Men would even attempt it? It [was] a total blast. If anyone out there ever contemplates a tour of any sort, I recommend taking someone with you. Because your job, out on the road, is to meet lovely strangers who've been kind enough to care enough to come out and say hello to you, and to be very, very present—and it's enormously helpful to have a person, like your mother, guiding your arm, and keeping an eye on the task at hand. ALSO, I would recommend taking MY mother with you. Because she's very funny, and it never hurts to have a gorgeous, glamorous woman with you, even if she does happen to be your mother.

The whole thing started off as a joke—in a marketing meeting with my publisher, I said, "Maybe I should bring my mother with me!" And no one laughed. Which taught me a real lesson. Namely, don't make jokes in marketing meetings, because they have a tendency to become PR strategies. So then, I called Mother, and said, "What do you think of the notion of heading off on the road with me?"

And she said, "I'll call you later, I'm going shopping."
Which is my mother's means of preparation. So she
got some gorgeous new suits, and adventure ensued.
It was very much like that Erik Preminger book about
being on the road with his mother, Gypsy Rose Lee. I
kept looking around, and there Mother was, sitting
cross-legged on the Vuitton suitcases, smoking, and
looking very glamorous and world-weary.

**When do you think your mother will write a book
about you?**

I only wish my mother would write a book about
ANYTHING! I'd be first in line to buy it—I feel like
my job in life is just to follow the genius, brassy
women in my family around with a pen, and write
down everything they say. My grandfather and I look
at each other all the time, and say, "How lucky are we
to be in the same room with these ladies!"

What are you working on now?

Well, I've got several pots on the stove. It looks like a
little picture book I did might be coming to
fruition... and I'm working on a sequel to my book.
And I have what I think is the most adorable idea for
a young adult series. But you know, there's that great
line about somebody saying to Baudelaire, "Mr.
Baudelaire, I have the most TERRIFIC idea for a
sonnet," and Baudelaire says, "Sonnets, sir, are not
made of ideas." And brother, you can say that again.
Sonnets, and anything like them, are made of hard,
slaving work. And as you know, hard work never gets
any easier. It's that awful, awful Zen thing about writing—how every time you sit down with blank paper,
you're beginning again. VERY humbling. Because
blank paper is no respecter of worldly success. And
you just have to keep returning to that desk every
day, and sometimes it's like going in for A Day of
Beauty at Elizabeth Arden, and sometimes, it's like
going to the salt mines.

When I was sixteen, my mother offered me fifteen hundred dollars if I swore never, ever to read her another poem I hadn't written. I cashed her check, but I've cheated once or twice. And the only time it's ever ended happily was when I discovered this poem, written by my super-hot friend Victoria Redel, from her book Swoon. *Mother says that more than anything she's ever encountered, this poem expresses the way she felt raising a gay son. It's very lovely, and I hope readers will love it, too.*

"Bedecked" by Victoria Redel

Tell me it's wrong the scarlet nails my son sports or
        the toy store rings he clusters
        four jewels to each finger.

He's bedecked. I see the other mothers looking at the
        star choker, the rhinestone
        strand he fastens over a sock.
Sometimes I help him find sparkle clip-ons when he
        says sticker earrings
        look too fake.

Tell me I should teach him it's wrong to love the
        glitter that a boy's only a boy
        who'd love a truck with a remote that revs,
battery slamming into corners or Hot Wheels
        loop-de-looping off tracks
        into the tub.

Then tell me it's fine—really—maybe even a good
thing—a boy who's got some girl
to him,
and I'm right for the days he wears a pink shirt on
the seesaw in the park.

Tell me what you need to tell me but keep far away
from my son who still loves
a beautiful thing not for what it means—
this way or that—but for the way facets set off
prisms and prisms spin up
everywhere
and from his own jeweled body he's cast rainbows—
made every shining true color.

Now try to tell me—man or woman—your heart was
ever once that brave.

"Bedecked"

Excerpted from *Swoon* by Victoria Redel.
© 2003 The University of Chicago Press
Reprinted with permission.

📖 Recommended Reading

Dearly Beloveds!

I tend to favor authors I'd like to have lunch with, so here's a whole party of good-time gals (and one great gay guy) for you to go raise hell and drink some margaritas with. Have fun, and write me at janeaustentexas@gmail.com when you're sober.

xx
Robert

I Capture the Castle by Dodie Smith

This is one of those jewel-box novels that's so entirely frustrating because it's so entirely unknown. Dodie Smith, whose fortune was made by her children's books (*101 Dalmatians*) wrote this wry and glorious romance about two poor sisters (in a castle!) with a graceful curtsy to Jane Austen. Trust me when I tell you you'll adore Cassandra and Rose. It's a novel that builds and builds like a locomotive, until it ends with a big, happy bang. Always a lovely thing.

Love in a Cold Climate by Nancy Mitford

Has there ever been anybody more charming and witty than Nancy Mitford? You know her, don't you? The one with all the sisters—one was a duchess, one was a communist, and two were Nazi sweethearts. Well, with material like that, how can a writer lose? This novel is chock-full of great lines, like when that awful ambassadress says she put India on the map. So wicked. Precious and priceless.

Hons and Rebels and A Fine Old Conflict by Jessica Mitford

Okay, so for those who don't know, these two memoirs were written by Nancy's little communist sister, and they just might be my favorite books of all time. Of course, they're both loaded with all that delightful Mitford madness, but they're also incredibly thoughtful and smart, packed with political adventure and intrigue, and funny, funny, funny.

Confessions of a Failed Southern Lady
by Florence King

Well, what can you say about the great Florence King? She's the only Republican lesbian feminist philosopher in the state of Virginia, and I can't help loving her dearly. She can, at times, be just *awful.* But she's forever brilliant and funny and besides, *Confessions* is also an incomparable story about growing up southern, female, and sane—all at the same time.

Molly Ivins Can't Say That, Can She?
by Molly Ivins

Molly Ivins made me so proud to be a Texan, and this collection of essays is my favorite of all her books. My mother and I still howl over the piece written about the Greenhouse, that fabulous Neiman Marcus salon outside Dallas, where a beautician, desperate to contrive a compliment, tells Molly she's got a fabulous space between her eyes. My friend Muriel Stubbs said, "You know, being smart and being intelligent isn't necessarily the same thing. But Molly was both." So true.

Faithfull by Marianne Faithfull

I wrecked my mother's car reading this book when I was sixteen. And not because I'm a lousy driver, but because this is an enthralling book, as addictive as the heroin that plagued dear Marianne. Partly because of its superior writing, but mostly because Marianne Faithfull is just such a badass. Hers is a big, unbelievable, mythic life, the least interesting part of which was that little star-crossed romance with Mick Jagger. I will admit that I'm not Marianne Faithfull, but it is not for lack of trying.

Eleanor Roosevelt, Vols. 1 & 2
by Blanche Wiesen Cook

And speaking of unbelievable, mythic lives... I
remember reading these books as a teenager and
thinking that if I could ever be half as good or brave
or strong as Eleanor, my life would be made, and
that's still the gospel truth. She is, to my mind, the
single greatest American.

D.V. by Diana Vreeland

Diana Vreeland—earthquaking editor of *Vogue*—was
one of those geniuses whose vision of the world was
so unique and profound that it absolutely changed
the way all of us live our lives. Don't you *dare* scoff;
it's the truth. She's right up there with Diaghilev,
Dior, and Disney, and she's also a ring-tailed blast.

Great Granny Webster and *The Last of the Duchess*
by Caroline Blackwood

The woman who wrote these two very different
books was an infamous beauty who enthralled and
married two very brilliant men—Lucian Freud and
Robert Lowell. She was also one hell of a terrific
writer who never, ever gets her due. High-minded,
elegant smut. You'll eat it with a spoon, and never
feel guilty.

Splendora by Edward Swift

For my finale, I'll round out with another perfect,
and perfectly unknown novel. It's my favorite Texas
book, and maybe, too, my favorite novel. It's a satire
and a fable about a little gay boy, Timothy John,
bruised and battered by his East Texas town, who
returns years later to reap his revenge disguised as a
lady of fortune, Miss Jessie Gatewood. It's a Texas
Twelfth Night with a happy ending! How high
the moon!

![] *Reading Group Questions*

1. What are some of your favorite of Mother's "quotable phrases" in *Memoirs*? Which of her words-to-be-embroidered did you find particularly funny, offensive, profound—or all of the above?

2. Robert spent most Saturday mornings at Neiman Marcus with Mother. What does he learn there about style and sophistication, art and artifice, and—most important—his identity? Discuss the department store as microcosm in Robert's world, and our own.

3. Take a moment to talk about Mother's desire for— and her attempts to be found desirable by—a wealthy new man. Do you believe she was desperate, or just deluded? Do you judge her for embodying the cliché of a Texas gold-digger? Or do you have sympathy for her as a so-called starter wife?

4. How do you feel about Daddy in *Memoirs*? Is he worthy of contempt? Or does he deserve forgiveness? What is your lasting impression of him, after the conversation he has with Robert on the phone?

5. What would have been different for Daddy and Mother has they given birth to a beautiful *girl* instead of Robert? Discuss your theories about what this family might have been like.

6. What does it mean to be "beautiful" in the context of this memoir? Is beauty skin-deep? Is it masculine or feminine? Coveted or feared?

7. How did Robert escape his small-town circumstances by joining the theater? In what ways— metaphorically and literally—does role-playing parallel one's coming-of-age? How did Robert eventually assume the role of his own true self?

8. Discuss the significance of Robert's dream in which he appears as a guest on the *Barbara Walters Special*, and Barbara tells him: "You're under the impression that the story of your life is your mother's story. But in time you'll realize that the story of your life is your own."

9. "My time in public school taught me the lesson every gay boy learns fast," writes Robert. "That language is the weapon of the powerless." Talk about Robert's path toward leading a literary life.

10. Now that you have read the material in this guide, do you feel differently about the author, or his mother? Were any of their insights surprising to you? How?